MW01105355

the good land

the good land

Stories of Saskatchewan People

PETER WILSON

FIFTH
HOUSE
PUBLISHERS

Copyright © 1998 Peter Wilson

All rights reserved. No part of this publication may be reproduced, stored in a retrieval system, or transmitted, in any form or by any means, electronic, mechanical, recording, or otherwise, without the prior written permission of the publisher, except in the case of a reviewer, who may quote brief passages in a review to print in a magazine or newspaper, or broadcast on radio or television. In the case of photocopying or other reprographic copying, users must obtain a licence from the Canadian Copyright Licencing Agency.

Front cover photograph by Peter Wilson

Cover and interior design by Brian Smith / Articulate Eye Design

The publisher gratefully acknowledges the support of The Canada Council for the Arts.

We acknowledge the financial support of the Government of Canada through the Book Publishing Industry Development Program for our publishing activities.

Printed in Canada.

98 99 00 01 02 / 5 4 3 2 1

CANADIAN CATALOGUING IN PUBLICATION DATA

Wilson, Peter (Peter Gordon), 1946–

 The good land

ISBN 1-894004-16-7

1. Saskatchewan—Biography.   2. Saskatchewan—Biography—Anecdotes. I. Title

FC 3505.W54 1998   971.24'009'9   C98-910808-2   F1070.8.W54 1998

Fifth House Ltd.

#9 - 6125 11 St. SE

Calgary, AB, Canada

T2H 2L6

1-800-360-8826

Contents

Front cover photograph

Born on a North Dakota farm in 1906, Irene Schultz moved to Saskatchewan with her family when she was eight years old. She never married, choosing to help work the family farm and take care of her aging parents until their deaths. When Peter Wilson stopped by in the spring of 1990, she told him that she never really had time to think about marriage. She supposed that was because she had been too busy over the years harnessing horses, milking cows, and putting up stooks to contemplate matrimony.

When Wilson met her, she was a sprightly 83-year-old, living alone in the same farmhouse that her father and uncle had built after the original family home had been destroyed by a terrific wind storm in the early '20s.

Living alone in an isolated farmhouse heated by a wood furnace and without running water, she said life was wonderful. She still kept a dozen or so sheep, which she fed and sheared, and spent her recreational time spinning wool and working in her garden, which Wilson recalls was the size of a mall parking lot.

She was very optimistic, a positive spirit in the universe. But it was her last words to Wilson as they said their goodbyes that stick in his memory. As she looked around towards the knurled black maple trees that lined her driveway, and then towards the empty fields that her family had farmed since almost the turn of the century, she turned to Wilson, who was already sitting in his car.

"Can you smell that?" she asked, breathing deeply. "There's another spring around the corner."

Dedication

For Deb, Marc, and Angeline, who keep the home fires burning.

Acknowledgments

There are so many roads in Saskatchewan: good blacktop highways, arrow-straight gravel roads, and dusty trails more suitable for hoof than tire. I think at one time or another I have got lost on most of them.

But, while it might not be too difficult to lose your way here, someone, somewhere will come along and find you, give you a meal, and, if you're lucky, tell you a story before they point you in the right direction home. That's the nature of this place and its people.

I am grateful to Fifth House Publishers, in particular its talented managing editor, Charlene Dobmeier, who, ever so patiently and with good humour, steered me through the tricky bits of putting this book together. I am also grateful to Sheila Bean for wielding her subtle and delicate editing skills with her usual merciless precision.

Special thanks to the Saskatoon *StarPhoenix*, my employer, for allowing me to explore Saskatchewan and for the encouragement and support the newspaper has offered me over the past 30 years.

FOREWORD

I love Saskatchewan. God's country, I call it. I grew up smack-dab in the middle of the bald prairie, where the land is as flat as your floor and the only trees were planted by hand, where there's no place to hide from the searing summer sun as it burns its way from one flat-line horizon to the other, where the wind sucks up all the moisture from the soil and from your skin, and where the winter cold is just plain dangerous. It's a fierce land.

This is the kind of place that breeds heroes. I'm not talking about puffed-up politicians or shiny rock stars or business sultans, even though Saskatchewan has spawned plenty of those. No, I'm talking about everyday heroes, the kinds of people who've looked the stark landscape and weather square in the eye, and have survived, and lived a good life, and might even still feel love for the place.

If you've ever lived in Saskatchewan, you know these people. They're farmers with big, strong fingers from a lifetime of milking cows. Long, sunny hours in the field have brought out speckles on their hairless heads. They're trappers and gold prospectors who really and truly understand what it's like to be alone, and sometimes lonely. They're people who are determined to preserve their ancestral traditions, from a spiritual journey in a sweat lodge to smooshing grapes for wine.

It's a real honour to know such fine folk, and you are about to meet some of them, thanks to Peter Wilson, a newspaper journalist who writes heartfelt, insightful stories and takes stunning photographs.

In 1968 Peter, then a young man from Yorkshire, England, was hired to take pictures for *The StarPhoenix* newspaper in Saskatoon. By the early 1980s his job had evolved into a mixture of writing and photography, and Peter's specialty was travelling all over this great province and collecting personal stories from a wide range of individuals.

Often he'd stumble across his subjects whilst on the trail of another story. For instance, he'd be interviewing a rancher about cattle feed and hear passing mention of Grandma, who lives down the road without electricity or plumbing. So he'd buzz over and interview Grandma. Or he'd be doing an interview in someone's home and admire the homeowner's assortment of salt-and-pepper shakers. "Oh, my," the homeowner would say, "my sister-in-law has a monstrous collection of these things." So he'd visit the sister-in-law.

I had the pleasure of working with Peter at the paper for nine years, and I have long admired his work. For starters, he's a brilliant photographer and a witty storyteller. More important, though, he's an excellent listener. Peter gives his subjects all of his attention and respect, taking in everything they say and noting their tone of voice, the way they hold their hands, and the expression in their eyes. While much of his work involves writing about the technical aspect of farms and farm machinery, Peter also has a special knack for zeroing in on people's thoughts and passions.

When Peter meets someone, he doesn't dismiss that person as an ordinary, uninteresting carbon copy of everyone else. Rather, he sees each person as an individual with a fascinating story to tell. An extraordinary story to tell. In this book you'll meet someone who breeds lynx for a living and someone who makes steamer models for a hobby. You'll hear heartwarming memories, of playing in a dance band, of herding cattle, and of making mincemeat from an Old Country recipe. And you'll talk philosophy (one nun is a hermit).

The common thread here? Simplicity, I guess. Either by choice or by circumstance, most of Peter's subjects have lived their lives without the luxury of money and sometimes without the joy of companionship. They've done without. They've worked like Trojans. Some have had the chance to live a more lush life, but instead have decided to focus on something they value more, such as the invigorating scent of the outdoors or the tranquil warmth of familiar hometown friends. Peter calls them "original souls," who've carved out their own lifestyle, perhaps under the scrutiny of others, perhaps in utter solitude. Maybe they've yet to achieve fame and fortune, but they have found contentment, their own daily rhythm, and possibly wisdom. Who could ask for greater riches?

So enjoy this book. Enjoy the friends you make here. Maybe your neighbours have a remarkable story to tell. Maybe you do, too.

Sheila Bean

Ferry and cable car belonging to Claudette and A.B. (Barr) Brookes.

Home across
the Water

He had given out the complex directions over the telephone on how to get to the family farm. "When you get to the water, beep your car horn, and I'll come over and get you."

It takes about four hours to reach Claudette and A.B. (Barr) Brookes' farm, 37 kilometres northwest of Meadow Lake. The medium of travel includes blacktop, gravel, dirt, and finally water—in the shape

1

of the Beaver River. It was the water part that interested me. Not everyone requires the use of their very own ferry to get home.

But that's what the owners of Brookes farm have been doing off and on since about 1919. That's when Barr's parents first came to this part of the country to raise cattle and settle the land.

Attracted by the rich hay meadows buried deep in dense bush and seeing the Beaver River as a reliable water source, the pioneers looked on this territory as pretty ideal cattle country. The area offered other advantages for would-be ranchers, as Arthur Brookes senior, Barr's father, recollected many years later. " ... north of the Beaver the land was unoccupied all the way from the Alberta border," he wrote in his memoirs.

As for the location, outside a few forest fires, a few serious floods, and the constant summer plague of flies and mosquitoes, they were not far wrong. Despite its occasional hazards, the river was a definite asset, says Barr.

The Beaver River's source is Beaver Lake, about 250 kilometres to the northwest in Alberta. It bends and curves like a convulsive snake to reach Ile-à-la-Crosse to help form the headwaters of the mighty Churchill River system in Saskatchewan's northland. Having land on both sides of the meandering waterway, the family found the Beaver proved quite a barrier to farm efficiency. While the river was low the cattle could ford the river to get to new pastures, but when the waters rose during spring runoff, or after a summer rain, there were problems. There was also a regular need to cross to get to the hay meadows, to cut and rake the crop for the cattle's winter feed.

So in those early days there was good reason for the Brookes family to build their first ferry. It was simple, but practical. Sturdy logs and stout rope secured the craft, and cables and ropes suspended between banks allowed the passengers to pull the ferry to the opposite shore.

All-in-all, developing a farm on the north side of the river seemed a good choice 70 years ago. That's when seasonal wagon trails or Indian hunting tracks were the only options for travellers. However, when roads were finally built in the region, the best ones happened to be on the south side.

The ferry took on more significance. Getting access to Meadow Lake's post office, stores, and medical services was more efficient using the more reliable road on the opposite side of the river.

And so, after peering over the edge of the bank that cut through the lush growth of river valley, I had beeped the car horn a couple of times to get my ferry ride.

Sure enough, the boxlike craft, with rancher-turned-skipper Barr Brookes at the helm, was slowly making its way to my side of the Beaver.

It looked as if it could easily hold a dozen passengers. His "ship" wasn't the *Queen Mary*, but with a wooden platform surrounded by waist-high railings it looked safe enough. What's more, buoyancy provided by a couple of plywood pontoons gave it a good two feet of freeboard; that's what really mattered.

"Come aboard," the 65-year-old rancher had yelled, lowering the gangplank—a couple of nailed 2x10s.

Barr Brookes pulled on the guide rope, and the green and red raft started back out across the Beaver River. Not a lot of pulling is required. The river is only about 125 feet wide, a big change from the average 175 feet it normally runs.

"Awful dry these past few years; never seen the Beaver this low," Barr said, heaving on the thick rope.

Barr and his father had built this ferry in 1959, and it's been running well since then. He pointed downstream to a series of cables about six metres above the slow-moving water. They ran parallel to the ferry's own guide wire.

"That's our cable car, another way we can get across the river," he said proudly.

The cable car, a wooden box that holds two kneeling adults, rests on small wheels that sit on the strong cables stretched across the river. The passenger pulls on a rope to move the vehicle to the far shore.

Barr explained that during the spring break-up and fall freeze-up the ferry is useless, so the 30-year-old cable car is put into service. It's also a useful backup when the ferry is anchored on the far side of the shore.

"My dad was originally from Northern Ireland. He had seen many of these types of cable cars in operation along the coast there. That's where he got most of his ideas."

The Brookes keep their two half-ton trucks parked on the south side of the Beaver. It doesn't take long to leave home, unhitch the ferry and pull yourself across the river. In not much more than five minutes Barr and I had crossed the narrow waterway, moored the craft and strolled up the bank that led to the Brookes' farm house.

The neat bungalow has been built around the original log house that Barr's parents built.

Claudette had set a table with fresh saskatoon muffins, homemade cookies, and steaming hot coffee.

"Oh, we might be isolated, but it doesn't stop us getting lots of visitors, although not as many as when the children were at home," Claudette said.

They had eight children and had felt the worry of their isolated location more than the kids. When Barr was a youngster, his mother, using correspondence courses, had given him his schooling at home on the farm. The looming importance of education, however, had meant different decisions had to be made for his own children.

"I knew what it was like to go without a proper education, and I wanted my kids to have proper schooling," says Barr.

One year river floods had put the ferry out of commission. For about six weeks Barr had to deliver his children to the school bus by motor boat. So in 1963, with their children aged from 6 to 18, they had moved to a home on the Beaver's south side. The Brookes ran their ranch and farm operation from a new home base.

"We had to think of the children's schooling, but after 10 years it was them who pressured us into coming back here," says Claudette. The youngsters enjoyed the river, played explorers and sea captains, and swam in the safe waters. It was an ideal place to raise kids, the couple agrees.

These days, with children gone, but a hundred head of cattle to take care of as well as numerous other livestock, the couple's lives are still full with many activities. The ferry and cable car continue to play a major role in the farm's success.

Picking up parts for the tractor, the twice-weekly run into Meadow Lake for mail, visiting neighbours, and completing the usual chores on their land on the other shore, they keep their ferry occupied.

"We use it all the time, maybe three times a day ... Other times it might be days before we need to go across ... But it's nice to know it's there if we need it," says Barr.

Most available wall space in Brian Hembroff's family room is filled with celebrity pictures.

Autographed Portraits
Cover Collector's Walls

W hat do Adolf Hitler, Mother Teresa, Neil Armstrong, and Nancy Reagan have in common? Well, outside their obvious eminence or notoriety, their other claim to fame is that their autographed portraits occupy equal space on the walls of Brian Hembroff's Regina home. The names of those famous and infamous figures might be interesting to history trivia buffs, but for avid autograph hounds, those collective names conjure up the challenge of building the ultimate collection.

Hembroff, a carpenter by trade, is also one of the province's most avid autograph hunters.

Talk about big-time name dropping. His bookshelves are dedicated to albums which hold hundreds of personally signed, glossy pictures of film, TV, and sports celebrities. Political heavy-weights such as Gerald Ford, Ronald Reagan, Brian Mulroney, and Pierre Trudeau smile reassuringly from the confines of the book. Big-time sluggers such as George Foreman and Muhammad Ali share pages with hockey greats and baseball superheros.

Hembroff has a definite link to the greats via his signatured photographs, but he says his hobby is much more than a desire to vicariously connect with these people.

"It's a hobby that has its challenges and its satisfactions. The people are out there somewhere, you know that, you just have to get your message to them," he explains.

It is in this foray of hunter and hunted that Hembroff's obvious skill leaps to the forefront. Most of us seeking autographs would write to the fan clubs, press officers, and public relations people who represent these folks. Not Brian Hembroff.

"That's the worst thing you could do. You just about guarantee getting a form picture—or worse, an auto-pen," Hembroff says disgustedly.

Faced with a veritable avalanche of requests, fan clubs and PR consultants, trying to satiate a fickle public's demand for photographic access to their clients, are understandably reluctant to tire the fragile wrists of their charges.

"Often you might get their secretaries forging their signatures. That makes them next to worthless to a collector."

However, he faces another, more sinister problem. The penetration of high-tech has infiltrated even this hobby with the coming of the auto-pen—the machine that reproduces the handwritten signature of the star.

The word auto-pen brings fear and dread to all collectors. How do you get around this encroachment of standardization? Hembroff says you have to find out where the stars hang their hats, baseball bats, or dancing shoes. You write to them in their homes or places of business.

But where do these folks hang out? Obviously in various penthouses, yachts, and miscellaneous villas around the more exotic regions of our world. Careful research and career watching reveal their home addresses, travel plans, and venue dates. Once you have tracked them down, what about the request? Does he say, "Send me an 8x10 autographed photograph of yourself pronto"? Well, not exactly.

"You have to be polite, and respectful, but you have to be honest not sucky. I write, tell them a little about myself and my family, and share a little of myself with them."

He never tells them he's a big-time collector. He says that would put them off, and it's tough enough getting autographs without shooting yourself in the foot.

It's not the easiest of hobbies when you reach the scale of Hembroff's operation. One year alone he wrote about 900 letters to the powerful and famous hoping for just a simple picture with an autograph scribbled across it.

"I get replies from most of the people I write to, but sometimes it can take quite a while for them to arrive," he says.

Sometimes if the stars are appearing in the province, he will do the back-stage routine to get autographs. But whether by letter, or waiting out in the cold, blowing on the tip of his ballpoint to keep the ink from freezing, it's all worth the wait.

That's because the stars come out every time Brian switches on the lights in his basement family room. Filling most available wall space, autographed photos of the Hollywood scene gaze down on this section of Regina suburbia.

"Sometimes I just come down here and sit with them," he says, fondly looking around his portrait gallery.

Hembroff says he doesn't make money at his hobby. Most of the trades he makes with other collectors are by way of exchange and barter.

There are always the missing autographs from any collection and Hembroff's is no exception. Fidel Castro and Bill Clinton are at the top of his hit list these days.

"I'll get Bill eventually. I think Fidel is still a bit of a long shot, but I have hope."

Jim Ternier uses an 80-year-old seeder inherited from his grandfather.

Farmer Makes
the Old Ways Work

The prairie wind catches his hair as he takes powerful strides across the summerfallow pushing the 80-year-old seeding machine.

The sight seems somewhat incongruous; ~~that,~~ backwards in this age of high-tech, most of the power used in Jim Ternier's commercial seed-growing operation comes from the 50-year-old's muscles.

On first inspection, life on Jim Ternier's farm appears to have taken an enormous leap backwards. In a world where bigger is supposed to be better, Jim's antique seeder and equally ancient hand-pushed cultivator work about two acres of land. Surprisingly the combination provides a decent living for his family.

For the last 10 years, while the focus of mainstream agriculture has centred on improving farm efficiency, using increasingly sophisticated machinery and chemicals, Jim has gone back to the land.

It might not be everyone's idea of an agri-business empire but Jim is a contented man. His methods of growing seeds organically on his property near Cochin, about 40 kilometres north of the Battlefords—with the same machinery used by his grandfather—has paid off.

Jim, his wife, Marie-Louise, and their three young children all get by quite comfortably on an income that amounts to little over $10,000 annually. Even with that limited income they still manage to buy the odd bottle of wine, and even make an occasional visit to Europe.

In fact, their 1,700-square-foot stuccoed home, overlooking the blue lake that creeps up to their land, has all the marks of prime recreational real estate. The topography and situation of the garden enterprise also make the place close to ideal for prairie seed growing. The slope of the hill and a tree belt offer protection from cold northerly winds. The waters of Murray Lake, that lap the shores of the Ternier property, provide a warming influence that minimizes the risk of early fall frost.

Varieties of beans, peas, corn, carrots, lettuce, spinach, squash, and a host of other garden favourites are grown on a sloping two-acre stretch of land that has been in the Ternier family for three generations.

Jim knows the land well, although he left the family farm in his late teens, first to study mathematics and then to travel the world. For about seven years he lived in France, where he worked as a gardener in an institution for mentally challenged adults. He returned to Saskatchewan and the family farm determined to make a go of living off the land. He began a market garden that later developed into his present seed operation.

A deep commitment to environmental protection means his operation is chemical-free. Ternier relies on leaving garden areas fallow to allow soil rejuvenation and relies on crop rotation to minimize the dangers of insects and crop disease. He even picks the potato beetles off his plants by hand.

Despite the lack of technological advancement, since he and his family moved back to his Cochin roots, there has been much progress during the last decade. That's reflected in the growing list of seed orders he gets every year from gardeners.

He says his annual income could rise to $12,000, but he doesn't sound overly excited about the prospect. What does excite him is his passion for collecting older varieties of vegetable seeds that early settlers brought from Europe.

Most of his business orders are generated from the seed catalogue he publishes, and while his regular customers are principally from Saskatchewan and Alberta, he has a sizeable clientele from coast to coast and even in the United States.

Although Jim performs much of the labour, the operation is very much a family enterprise. Despite her busy life as a university student, where she's studying to become a pastoral counsellor, Marie-Louise helps produce their annual seed catalogue.

The family budget is closely monitored and augmented by a heart-felt philosophy of self-sufficiency. Their food supply is either grown by themselves or purchased from local producers. It also doesn't hurt that Jim has a penchant for selecting used clothing for himself instead of buying new duds, and has an aversion to any form of bank loan.

It all works out to be a simple lifestyle, but one that seems to ensure continued solvency, a tough act these days for most people who work the land.

Sister Susanne chooses to live her life alone.

Nun Travels
Solitary Spiritual Path

It was quite a trudge hiking through the soft snow to get to the hermit's tiny cottage. Sister Susanne Mowchan, however, with 18 winters of following the same path, had little difficulty negotiating the rough route across the field leading to her home.

I was visiting one of my favourite haunts in the province—St. Peter's Abbey at Muenster, about an hour and a half drive east of Saskatoon. This time I was not talking to the friendly Benedictine monks at the monastery. I was seeking out a woman who had chosen the spot to spend her life alone—a hermit—in search of spiritual fulfilment.

Struggling along the snowy bank behind her, I thought of the spiritual path that this nun had travelled since leaving her Pennsylvania convent almost two decades earlier. Sister Susanne was 18 when she entered the convent in Columbia, near Harrisburg. She'd put in a year working for the state government as a secretary, although she'd known all along that she would eventually enter the convent.

"My parents were a little concerned about my idea of becoming a nun, so I agreed that after finishing high school I would spend a year working in an office," Sister Susanne told me.

And it was a year, to the day, that she handed her notice to her surprised boss and the next day drove over to the convent. The move, however, was very predictable to the teenager; she'd been five years old when she had embraced the idea of becoming a nun.

"In the small town where I was born I remember the nuns coming to pick up my elder brothers to take them off to regular catechism lessons. I wanted to go along so bad I cried, but of course I was too young," the 53-year-old sister recalls.

Through tear-filled eyes she watched the nuns drive away, but suddenly the young girl felt a wonderful peace descend on her. From that moment the world seemed brighter and she was "engulfed by God's presence." Even at such an early age she knew where life would lead her. The call from God was that simple and that definite.

"Strange place to end up. In Saskatchewan, I mean," I said to her, straying off the narrow path in my attempts to keep up, and sinking thigh deep into wet snow.

"Not really," she said, smiling at my predicament with the unfamiliar terrain. "To me it's exactly the right spot."

We passed a sign nailed to a power pole that more or less informed the curious they were about to enter a hermit area. Avoidance was suggested.

Sister Susanne had agreed to talk with me, to explain a little about her reasons for being here, and to show off the tiny hermitage on the monastery grounds where she spends her days and nights.

Out here, squeezed between tall spruce trees on one side and empty prairie on the other, Sister Susanne could not have found a more secluded spot to continue building her religious life. Of course, rational thought would follow that if you chose the life of a hermit, the words solitary, isolated, and aloneness would hold a certain resonance. The appeal of living under those conditions, which would allow her greater opportunity to listen and talk to God, made it an easy decision to move from her convent home in the U.S. to the Canadian prairies.

"I was teaching grade school at the convent, but my heart was somewhere else. I was very much drawn to the life of a hermit."

Water dripped from the roof of the hermitage and I took a peek at the back of her house. A small flower garden, buried in the snow, merged with the cluster of dense trees. Beyond the trees, about 600 metres away, lay the hidden, stately monastery of St. Peter's. In the garden, a bird feeder and bird bath—a wide bottomed fry-pan full of water—were attracting signs of spring on the wing. The birds were the only signs of movement in this peaceful place.

I followed Sister Susanne inside. Taking my wet boots off in the closet-sized porch, I walked into the hermit's kitchen/office, which was about the size of the smallest bedroom in an average three-bedroom bungalow. The place was as neat as a pin. In the centre of the room was the main piece of furniture, a large desk. A couple of folding chairs, a sink unit, and some kitchen cupboards lining the wall made up the rest of the furniture and fittings in the simple room. Religious pictures hung on the walls and a few spiritual books made their home in a cardboard box bookcase perched on the desk, ready for easy access.

"Where do you eat?" I asked, looking around for a table.

She reached over and triumphantly pulled out a sliding writing tray that was hidden under the desk. Her dining table was the size of a cutting board. Obviously the social calendar is not a major concern for a hermit.

*Brian Stang watches as his cousin Michael (both 13) tests
his throwing arm for upcoming bunnock competition.*

Horse Bones Are Used
to Play Bunnock

I f you've a keen eye, a steady arm, and a yen for some big dollars in
prize money, you should heed the town of Macklin's call of "Let's
play bunnock." Taking sharp aim with a horse's ankle bone could
put you in line for a $2,500 first prize in the World Championship
Bunnock competition.

We all understand prize money, but what in heaven's name is bunnock?

Well, you have to start with a whole bunch of horse ankle bones to get a true idea of the sport.

This is no leg-pulling exercise, Rudolph Stang told me. The Macklin area farmer, and one of the event's organizers, says the sport is very popular in a few German-settled communities in the province.

He explained to me that bunnock is a team competition with four players on each side, using horse ankle bones. The object is to knock down the opponent team's line of 22 bones with your thrower bones.

"As far as we know the game originated in Russia. It was brought over here when German families, who had lived in Russia for many years, moved to Canada at the beginning of the century."

A full game of bunnock uses 52 bones. The eight heaviest are called shoniesers, or throwers, while four are marked as guards. The rest make up the formation of ordinary soldiers, which get knocked over by the throwers as the game progresses.

Stang remembers playing the game with his father, and in turn taught his own children how to play it. He says that while the game never seemed to catch on outside the small towns where it began, it is a strongly practised recreation where it's survived. His youngest son Brian, eight, provides some healthy competition for his dad out in the front yard these days.

"This event should put bunnock on the map and hopefully spread knowledge and appreciation of the game," he told me.

Organizers in this bustling oil-patch community near the Alberta border, about 250 kilometres west of Saskatoon, hope to attract more than 75 teams to their world championships, some from as far away as Edmonton and Calgary. Outside the fun of the competition, a $5,000 chest of prize money sweetens the pot considerably, and should attract a hefty number of entries, says Stang.

The game combines the skills of bowling and skittles with the military strategy of chess. The fact you play it with horses' ankle bones also adds some sense of history to the pastime.

"In the old days, when horses did the heavy work on farms, the prairie was littered with the dead animals' ankle bones. You had no trouble finding them around," Stang says.

These days, with tractors taking over the burdens of farm tasks, horses are few and far between, particularly dead ones. Now players have to rely on horse-owning neighbors, or the few abattoirs that specialize in processing horse meat.

"They are also starting to manufacture bones out of plastic material; we'll have to see how they work out," says Stang.

Herb Seesequasis with grandsons Everett Cameron (left) and Craig Cameron.

The Sweat Lodge ——— Is a Testament to Faith ———

E xcept for the glow of the red-hot rocks in the centre of our circle, it was very, very dark. It must have been the depth of the darkness that made the staccato noises of the Indian rattle feel, rather than sound. In the blackness, and in the confined space of the sweat lodge, the sharp noise felt as if it came from inside my chest rather than from its actual source.

There were 12 of us inside the sweat lodge, a spiritual cocoon made from a skeleton of bent willow branches covered with thick tarp. We were on the Beardy's Reserve near Duck Lake, about an hour's drive from Saskatoon.

I was not very comfortable. My spine bent to the same arch as the tent.

My crossed legs were disturbingly close to the fire rocks. In the lodge, in the darkness, we were all together and all alone.

Shaking the hide-covered rattle, prayer leader Herb Seesequasis was gathering the attention of the angels, or grandfathers as they are known in this other world. We were a group, a congregation, gathered to travel under a suffering blanket of steam and heat to communicate with a world outside my usual reality. We were seeking the eternal.

In the dark, I heard the spitting of cool water hitting the hot rocks and felt the slow envelope of steam beginning to rise around me. Then the singing began. The heat and the rhythmic high and low notes from the 12 voices quickly took up all space outside myself and began to penetrate inwards.

As more water hit the fire circle, the temperature rose. Led by Herb, voices moved in practised tones and sounds to collect all our thoughts, hopes, and fears, and in our collective noise direct them towards the grandfathers.

Only the grandfathers can talk to God; we are not worthy, says Seesequasis, a Cree medicine man. The sweat lodge serves to heal all wounds. And it's true, emotions and physical ailments feel the weight of millenniums of focused spirituality. The people come to sweat and to pray to a higher power, and the haunting music from the gathered voices is no less pure for its humble surroundings.

The flap of the lodge was lifted, flooding the place in light, but a fog of steam allowed only a translucent visibility. Eagle feathers, special herbs, and sweetgrass play their role in the ritual. A peace pipe went around. We smoked and turned the long pipe stem clockwise, representing a neverending circle, and passed it to our companion in our own circle of faith.

The flap went down once again and a new round of sweat and prayers began. There would be four rounds in all. Each time, new hot rocks were added in the fire circle and the progressive sweats became hotter.

Once there was a time, says Herb, when European religion outlawed the sweat lodge and its traditional customs. They didn't realize the Indians sent their prayers to the same God, he said with a smile.

In this sweat, Herb had two of his young grandchildren participating. There is no way the sweat lodge will die out, he says forcefully, not if he has anything to do with it. You can't kill such a deep need, he says.

He is a modest man and takes no credit for what he does. A simple ceremonial gift of ribbon, cloth, or tobacco serves as the only entrance fee to his sweat lodge. He has seen many cures in the 17 years he has been a medicine man. Now he's 59 and will make sweats for many others over the years. He's here to help.

But it's really God who does the work, God and the grandfathers, he explains. In this cathedral of willow and canvas, faith knows only its own barriers.

Watchmaker Bob Strohan in the organized confusion of his small store.

This Doc Finds Time
to Make House Calls

H e's called the Tic Doc, or at least that's the name above the storefront in the old City Hall Mall in downtown Regina. I'd popped into the store to get a new battery for my watch. After being 20 minutes late for an appointment with a colleague, thanks to a slow watch, I figured it was about time for the right time. That's when I met the Tic Doc.

The name of the watchmaker and store owner is Bob Strohan. He's a large imposing fellow, made even more imposing by a strikingly wonderful beard that flows below his chin like a rich vine. He's also known as the Tic Doc, and while he's no medical doctor, the complex order in the anatomy of clocks and watches is as familiar to him as his own social security number.

Surrounded by the individual impassive faces of what looks like the entire watch and clock population of greater Regina, Strohan and his two assistants (one is his wife, LaVaughn) squeeze behind the store's counter/workbench. Organized confusion is what he calls the general state of his small store.

Awaiting attention, minute and bulky miscellaneous parts sit like pieces of a particularly frustrating jigsaw puzzle. Gears, springs, screws, and a thousand what's-its sparkle under the strong work lights that illuminate the bench. But this is no watch graveyard, no cemetery for dead clocks. These pieces will all eventually find their way back home to a proper and rightful body.

"Never had a watch come in here I couldn't fix," Strohan says matter-of-factly.

With his magnifying lens attached to his spectacles, tiny delicate instruments held rock-steady in his hand, and an eye that focuses as unwavering as a laser beam, Strohan looks every bit the image of his profession. Not surprising, since he was born into it. His father was a watchmaker, and since he was six, Tic Doc has been fixing the busted and dusty innards of the nation's timepieces.

"My parents used to put me up on a high bench, give me a watch to work on and leave me to it. That was the way they used to babysit me," he told me.

It was a method of child raising that might not have been a big hit with Doctor Spock, but for the young Strohan it proved rewarding. From the moment he took his first squint at the tightly coiled springs and shiny brass wheels of a watch's insides he knew where time would lead him.

From an original store in Prince Albert to others in Calgary, Strohan moved with his folks, building up his knowledge of the tricks and secrets of watch repair. He also slowly developed the patience and natural curiosity that are the real trademarks of all good watchmakers.

"You see a timepiece that doesn't work as a challenge. Getting it back into good working order feels like solving a mystery to me," says Strohan, who settled in Regina 26 years ago.

Rolex, Timex, and Sungsport. Mechanical, quartz, or electronic. Strohan has seen lots of changes in design and technology over his 51 years. However, while time machines might be able to change their spots over the years, for Tic Doc, a watch is a watch is a watch.

"They are all designed to do the same job. My work is to get them to perform that task accurately and for a long time."

Not that he restricts himself to fixing only wristwatches. Clocks of every size and dimension fall under his eagle eye. And if the clock's too big, this doc makes house calls. He'll travel to jobs wherever time has stood still.

"I've worked on the big post office clocks in places as far away as the Battlefords, Weyburn, and Melville, but these are on a kind of different scale."

That's for sure. Some of these beauties have gears in them the size of an average sedan's front wheels. But the machines work on the same principle as the old alarm clocks sitting next to your ear on the night stand.

Life might ebb and flow, but time marches relentlessly on, and that's good for business.

"It's a great job. I've never wanted to do anything else. Coming to work is still fun for me, and I'll probably keep on doing what I'm doing while my eyes and hands still work."

Of course, there's a drawback to the watchmaker's life. Tic Doc can never use the excuse most of us cling to when we sleep in, or arrive late for that important scheduled appointment. Since the beginning of time the rest of us have been able to rely on the old well-worn statement, "Sorry I'm late, damned watch must be slow."

Pansy White enjoys the freedom and independence of running her own ranch.

The Good Land
of Pansy White

I t's quite the view. On a clear day, looking southwest from the high plateau, you can see all the way to the Sweet Grass hills of Montana, 100 kilometres away.

This clear day, however, the keen 73-year-old eyes of Pansy White were set in another direction. Her proud gaze centred on a particular plump Limousin calf standing among the rest of her 80 head—munching and chewing their way below the broad ridge.

"There it is. I'm right particular proud of that one. It looks like a film star, don't it?" she laughs. Aiming her four-wheel-drive half-ton into a coulee, steep enough that the uninitiated might wish for an attached bungee cord, she rides in hot pursuit of the muscle-bound critter.

Pansy has run the White Mud Ranch single-handed since she took over from her dad, almost 25 years ago. Outside the help of neighbours, who can be relied on to help during the busy branding and haying seasons, the energetic rancher manages her spread alone.

For seven decades the coulees and hills, which sweep the horizon like ocean swells, have been her home. The 2,700 acres of ranch land where she runs her beloved cattle are a big part of her. It's all very personal, with the topography of this sparse and lonesome land acquiring the individual I.D. usually saved for human connections. Front, Stable, Muddy Knoll, Stone Ridge; the hills and coulees around the spread are treated with the same familiarity and love as her grandchildren.

"Some years back a cow died in a snow slide, so we named that place Reddy, after the cow."

Not that she puts her land or cattle before her real family. With a daughter, three granddaughters, and 10 great-grandchildren, the walls of her comfortable ranch house are crowded with family photographs. Often her great-grandchildren, who live in more urban settings, take time out to visit and spend a few days on the ranch.

"They love to travel down and spend time with me. It's good experience for them and a good excuse to get to know each other."

One thing's for sure, there's never a shortage of four-legged transportation on the ranch. With nine horses, a pony, and a donkey in the corral, Pansy could form her own posse if she had to.

However, more often than not Pansy prefers to use her truck when it comes to riding the range. Repairing fences and caring for her cattle means pastures must be checked regularly, sometimes four wheels can be better than four legs.

"I use a horse less and less as I get older, but I still ride horse when I'm not in a big hurry. The truck seems easier nowadays, and you can get a lot more baler twine and fence posts in the back."

But the landscape is still pure cowboy country. Thirty kilometres south of Maple Creek you're temporarily out of wheat fields and into serious ranching property. The land is reluctant to produce much, except for prairie grass and sage, and then only enough that it takes 30 acres of grazing cover to sustain a single cow, says Pansy.

If it hadn't been for the water supply, and the creeks that flow out of the nearby Cypress Hills, her parents would have given the place a wide berth. Instead they gambled their luck with the other pioneers who settled the region early in the century. The settlers desperately counted on the sometimes fickle water supply from those creeks. The Belanger, Sucker, Farewell, and the White Mud creek brought life to their lands.

Pansy still counts on the spring floods from these creeks to irrigate her hay flats and to supply her cattle with water; before the streams move on towards the Frenchman River, and eventually into the Missouri on the long journey to the Gulf of Mexico. No one takes water for granted around these parts.

After showing off her prize new calf Pansy manoeuvres the Ford around a ravine, immediately spotting an antelope a couple of kilometres away on the side of a distant hill.

"There's lots around nowadays, but I don't go after them anymore."

One time, she hunted these hills. The wild meat was a welcome change from the steady beef diet she was used to. On the shelves of one of the dressers in her home there's evidence she still handles a gun. Next to crowded bric-a-brac and memorabilia a few shotgun shells and 30/30 bullets stand like miniature bookends.

"My poultry gets bothered by coyotes once in a while, so I have to shoot off the gun occasionally to keep them at a distance."

Her father moved from England as a lad of 15. Lured by the romanticism of tales of the wild west, he travelled to the middle of nowhere. He needed all that young enthusiasm to stick it out, but stick it out he did. He and his wife made enough of a living on their homestead to provide well for their three children.

"It was a good life. We worked hard on the chores but we had lots of good times."

Her scrapbooks show the black-and-white images of a long ago time. Saddle horses with confident children astride. Big pulling horses overshadowing the tiny hands that hold the reins. Horses in corrals and horses on the range. Big horses and little horses, big kids and little kids; all enjoying each other's company.

"Now I'm the only one. My brother and sister are both dead now."

She was married for a time but it didn't last. "I guess we weren't a good match so we went our separate ways." Pansy came back to the family ranch in the early '60s to farm alongside her parents. When they died she decided to continue on, operating the ranch solo.

"Well, what else was I supposed to do? I enjoyed it, and was fair good at it so I stayed at it. That's where I am today," she says, bringing the big truck to a stop.

Satisfied blue eyes sparkle in her sun-bronzed face as she takes in the wide panorama. Besides her cattle and horses, the ranch is home to a couple of dozen geese, ducks, and turkeys as well as two dogs and a young cat with five kittens in tow.

"I like all livestock, including the pet variety. I even allow the cat indoors if she's good."

Despite her relative isolation, she's not short of creature comforts. The original family piano, delivered on a high-sided wagon when her parents settled here, still stands in the living room. On the wall next to it there's a fancy decorated guitar.

"I sent for it when I was a teenager. I paid for it with the money I made selling coyote pelts I'd hunted with my hounds."

There wasn't much time for schooling; her main education came naturally alongside her life on the ranch. Calving and branding cattle seemed more important back in those early prairie days.

"It's different now. Kids need a good education if they want to get anywhere, if they want any choices out of life. Me, well I've made my choice and I can't say I made a bad one."

Where she's parked her truck the cattle, far in the distance, look like toys as they graze quietly across the hillsides. The dome sky stretches over the countryside forever. Living here you live close to the seasons.

By early summer, if the spring rains come, the prairie grasses will drift to green and wildflowers can glow like painted buttons. But the landscape, like her human companions, colours itself more seriously with age.

Generally by mid-September brown and grey splash the steep hillsides and only the sunset relieves the sombre pattern. This year is different. She's never seen a year so wet and everything staying this green. But that's what's so good about living here; there are always surprises.

"I can't say winter troubles me, but I welcome spring. We need the summer's heat and by fall we're too busy to think much of anything. You can't beat living out the seasons right here."

Lorrie Reed helps a sheep off with its winter coat.

Sheep-shearing
Is Back-breaking Work

Contrary to popular opinion, sheep do not say baaaaa, they say mirrrr. At least that's the sound Peter and Pam Gonnet's sheep let rip on the PFRA pasture Peter manages near Broderick, south of Saskatoon. Last week was sheep-shearing time for the Gonnets, who own about 57 head of Suffolks and Cheviots, and the sound of mirrrrs was everywhere.

The racket was echoing mostly around the small barn, which doubled as the shearing hut. Inside the barn, penned in a small corral, the sheep waited for the clippers. Two at a time, they were persuaded into a couple of temporary shearing stalls set up within mirrrring distance of the pen.

While Peter, with the help of a neighbour, pushed, prodded, and cajoled the nervous sheep, trying to separate the reluctant beasts to be shaved from the crowded herd, the shearer's cutters whirred constantly.

Lorrie Reed has been shearing other people's sheep for about three years. Before that, he learned his skills on the small herd he raises on his farm near Elrose. The custom work helps supplement Reed's regular farm income, which is suffering through the worldwide dip in agricultural prices.

Reed is busiest from March through June as he tries to handle his own farm chores while visiting other operations, where he might be called to handle anywhere from 5 to 100 sheep at each location.

Reed and the two extra workers he has hired will be expected to shear 83 sheep at the Gonnet place. Some of the couple's neighbours have brought their own sheep to take advantage of Reed's visit.

An electric motor that powers the cutters hangs from the low rafters of the barn. Each crew member takes an average of about six minutes to shear a sheep. When Reed has felt like testing himself, he has managed to cut that time considerably. Taken against an experienced Australian shearer, he admits even his best time is slow motion. He says Down Under they can whittle the time to 90 seconds.

It's all in the action and method. The sheep is none too delicately uprooted into a sitting position. Sitting on its rear end, with front legs and head tucked under the shearer's arm, the animal immediately becomes docile. There is barely a mirrrr.

While it seems easier than might be expected on the animals, the human side to the equation fares less well. It's back-breaking work. Stooped over hour after hour, back muscles become taut and then numb. It's only during periodic breaks that the worker gets to straighten up and stretch to reclaim his painful muscles.

As the shearers remove the thick coat from each sheep, the fallen wool is gathered up by Pam Gonnet. She puts armfuls into giant-sized jute bags. As the sheep follow the assembly line, more and more wool starts to pile up in the bags. Pam has to climb inside them to compress the wool with her feet. By the time the bag is full, Pam's woollen base has gained her more than a metre in height and her head rubs against the barn roof.

She says each sheep gives up about five to eight pounds of wool, depending on the size of the animal. It is shipped off to an Alberta plant for cleaning and preparation. By the time it gets back, it will be ready to add a little more value to the Gonnet income.

Pam makes crafts from the wool. Seat covers for trucks and cars and cushions for kitchen chairs form the biggest part of her output. It's not big business, more a hobby really, but the final results are impressively luxurious.

And the good thing is sheep don't seem to mind parting with their woollen overcoats that grew thick through the winter. However, emerging from the darkness of the barn into the bright light of the pasture, they do look somewhat unsure of themselves.

Maybe not wiser, but for sure a whole lot lighter, they pick their way around the spring puddles and head towards the feed bin. Looking a little like stagehands in a Gary Larson cartoon, all they have left is their lamb linguistics to express a few mirrrrs of complaint here and there.

Sharon and Andy MacKenzie, with Donna, 2, and Melody, 5,
"live with the Lord and he provides for us."

Faith and Hard Work Provide
— a Simple but Rewarding Life —

resh bread was cooling in the kitchen. I noticed the satisfying aroma as I followed Andy MacKenzie into his home in this tiny community, west of Elrose. He had just finished a morning's work removing ceiling tiles from a soon-to-be-demolished home in this rapidly shrinking hamlet. While he had worked in the old house his wife, Sharon, had baked a half-dozen whole wheat loaves.

"There was a time when this town had two stores, two garages, a pool hall, and elevators," he said. At 39, he's too young to remember the boom years of this community, but he's listened to the old-timers of the district relive their past.

His two young children—blonde-haired blurs—ran and anchored themselves, one to each of his legs as he walked into the room. Leaning down he gave them a collective hug.

"We have another but she's away at school," said Sharon, automatically setting another place at the table. "You will stay for some lunch?" she asked.

Times are tough in rural Saskatchewan. Foreclosures, farm bankruptcies—the malaise has thrown many families into emotional turmoil. There is a real fear running throughout the province's heartland. But there's also a toughness that comes from hard practice dealing with fate that, at least lately, has been less than neutral. The MacKenzies face their future with courage, the courage born with an unshakable faith in their God.

The exodus from the countryside to the dubious security of the city has sucked the lifeblood from many of Saskatchewan's small communities. Wartime has suffered its own way through the ups and downs. Today, with a population hovering around a dozen, a bustling metropolis it isn't. More folks have left than arrived since its boom days.

The MacKenzies moved here in 1986 from the nearby farmhouse they had been renting. Their roots are close. Andy was born just a few kilometres from the hamlet and Sharon was raised near Eatonia, less than 100 kilometres down the highway from the front door of her Wartime home.

"We paid $4,000 for this house. That's one thing about rural living these days. Real estate is cheap," Andy says, spreading butter on a thick slice of bread.

With the farm economy in such bad shape, how does he manage to survive in this almost-empty hamlet?

"I hold down quite a few jobs," he answers, chuckling. "I'm a preacher for our local congregation in Eston, I drive schoolbus in the winter, I paint and shingle houses when the work comes along, I'm the pest control officer for the RM, and I also keep a few bees."

Faith in themselves and in their God, and a will to spend their days in the place where their roots run deep, make for a simple but rewarding life.

"I think wanting too much gets people into trouble. We have very little in a material sense. I don't buy into the destructive merry-go-round or feel a need to compete with my fellow man," Andy says.

Before our lunch Andy spoke a quiet prayer of thankfulness while the family lowered their heads. His were simple words of gratitude: thanks for the food, for the good health, for their security, and for the companionship of this stranger who was no longer a stranger. It was a peaceful refuge from the slings and arrows whistling around outside. God was in his heaven and all was well with the world. It's a theme that has paid off for this family, at least.

Little has changed at the Clear Spring colony since
Peter Wilson took this photograph in 1989.

Hutterites Live Communally
to Survive

Being addicted to radio news, I'd heard all about famine, blood-shed, and the black-edged world economy on my 120-kilometre drive to buy my festive goose.

The news was depressing. I needed cheering up. Maybe that's why I'd picked the Clear Spring Hutterite Colony near Kenaston to buy the bird I was going to cook for the New Year's dinner. My supplier was certainly a lot farther away than the local Co-op, but there's something about this rural spot that defies the regular world order. I had first discovered the colony back in 1989. A colleague and I were privileged to spend some time here researching a feature story on Clear Spring and its people.

It was quite a while since I'd been in the Kleinsasser parlour, but nothing had changed. The clock was the same, the three or four thermometers spread across the walls were all in place; more important, Susie and Chris Kleinsasser were still the same. Like the functional homemade furniture that stood around the edges of the small room, Susie and Chris were the picture of tough, solid confidence. Their faces reflected a deep faith—faith in their God and faith in their ability to survive.

Survival is something Hutterites have long since grown used to. Through history, persecution has knocked the Hutterites from Czechoslovakia to Hungary, Romania, Russia, and finally into North America. It seems pacifism, joint ownership of property, and communal living don't sit well with some people.

At Clear Spring they eat in community, pray in community, and work in community. The community is the administration centre, party headquarters, and emotional bosom of the 80 or so people who live here. The people live and work so the colony, and thus themselves, can survive. Whether that involves attending regular religious services, seeding fields, taking care of their elderly, or raising a flock of geese, residents fit snugly into their respective places in the colony's jig-saw puzzle. And it seems to work. A spiritual trust in God, and a more down-to-earth reliance on each other provides security in both this world and the next.

The Kleinsassers' young grandchild, Linda, walked into the parlour weighed down with the plucked, packed, and frozen goose I was buying. Shy but smiling, she swung the big bird down from her shoulder for me to ponder. Everybody learns about the work ethic in the colony.

The essence of life for a Hutterite is based on prayer, work, and simplicity. Simple black clothes, black boots, and the broad-brimmed black hat are the functional fashion trademarks of the men.

However, a scarf, a shirt, or the high-top sneakers—worn by the more daring Hutterite kids, highlight a contrast in both image and personality. Like the calendars sent by hopeful implement dealers, which often provide the only colour decoration in a colony's rooms, the Hutterites' dress code has a carefully controlled splash of colour in its wardrobe.

I reflected on the familiarity of the scene as I drove away with the frozen goose in the trunk of my car. How little things seemed to have changed. The steam was billowing out of the long hog and chicken barns just like the first winter I visited. The kids still tobogganed on the same hill, and the same black-clothed figures made their way to church, the dining-room, or the community root cellar.

In a world where we are badgered into accepting change as inevitable, it's wonderful to observe a rich denial of that world reality at some level. Sure they keep up with modern farm practices, buy sophisticated equipment, but the Hutterites' social values seem to stay the same.

Change in our society has all too often become cloaked in self-righteousness. It has become almost necessary and sacrosanct in the rush towards the hallowed halls of progress. I personally hold no grudge against change; some of it has been downright good for me. But I have this nagging thought that sometimes change does have the nasty habit of becoming all too familiar. Take a historical look at the changing situation in the Balkans or check out the tribal struggles in Somalia.

The radio news broadcast on the return journey held similar messages of chaos and mayhem erupting around our uncertain world. However, this time it wasn't quite as depressing. I was too distracted wondering how to cook my own goose this New Year.

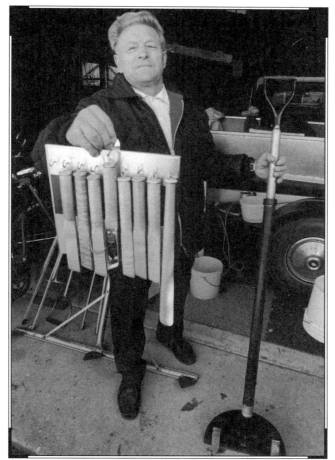

William Manke is the father of invention.

Inventiveness
Born of Poverty

His finger moved over the sensitive trap door in the little box, and the sharp snap reverberated around the packed garage. William Manke was building a better mousetrap.

If necessity is the mother of invention, then surely Manke, a retired railwayman, has to be the father. Judging by all the projects and designs that lie around his garage, shed, and Preston Avenue home, the 72-year-old Manke probably could design round pegs to fit snugly into square holes.

From extension apple pickers to litter grabbers, mechanical garden edgers to irrigation systems, bike buggies to fish scalers—there's original equipment made from scratch by Manke that fits the bill and task at hand. You can find these tools, purposeful devices, and many more creations that sprang from the depths of Manke's fertile mind, occupying every inch of space on his shelves.

Saskatchewan has produced its fair share of talent over the years. Many of the so-called stubble jumpers are now lining the boardrooms and factories of major corporations and government agencies across the country. All of them have managed to build their equivalent of better mousetraps over the years.

However, Manke, like most of us, didn't make the big time. Cherrywood boardroom tables, fat expense account lunches, and yachts in the Grand Caymans were not on the script for his future.

Born into the Dirty Thirties amid all the dust, heat, and poverty, Manke discovered his talents in the worthwhile process of survival.

"Nine years of no crops," he says, and in one short sentence sums up the frustrations and suffering that gave birth to his inventiveness.

He still has one of the weasel traps he designed and built as a child on the Estevan-area farm where he grew up. Before he hit his teenage years, he was catching live weasels in his traps and feeding them until winter came. That way he would have the more valuable white fur to bargain with. Muskrats and gopher tails added to his income.

"It was the only way we could make any cash money. They were hard times."

He was 15 when he moved away from the impoverished family farm. First he found work with other farmers. They put a roof over his head and food in his belly for a full day's work. After a number of labouring jobs, he began a career on the railroad. He eventually moved to Saskatoon and found work at the university in the crop science department.

He's been retired a long time now but the extra time on his hands has not been wasted. His active brain has come up with ideas that turn busted hockey sticks into apple pickers, and scrap steel and used lumber concoctions become specialized garden implements.

If there's one drawback to his agile mind and skilful hands, it's that Manke has a tough time staying still.

"If I don't have a task or a job to do, I start to get a little agitated and restless. I guess I need to be busy all the time, but that gets things done," he says.

So when he completes one project—such as the electric coffee grinder that's now modified to turn out breakfast cereal, or a bicycle buggy that can carry several hundred pounds of weight—he quickly moves to a new objective.

Lately, his thoughts are turning to a pet project that's been hanging around in the back of his mind for a long time. He talks out loud as he explains the features of his new invention.

"Well, it will need a supersensitive spring, and a ramp because there's need to get some extra elevation." His speech picks up speed as the picture of the new device takes shape in his brain.

"Then there will be the small water tank, and the bait tray ... "

Another, and even better mousetrap is beginning to take shape on Preston Avenue.

Phil Foster loves his new life as a northern outfitter.

His Fishing Camp
Is Close to Paradise

Warm thoughts of his Saskatchewan fishing camp carry Phil Foster through the long winter months of the Colorado construction season.

"After I've had a really bad day, where everything seems to have gone wrong, folks wonder how come I have a smile or a stupid grin on my face. That's when I tell 'em about this place," he told me.

"This place" is the Koo Sto Wilderness Camp, a fly-in fishing camp on the remote shores of Lower Foster Lake, about 120 air miles north of La Ronge.

The 28-year-old Foster had dropped in—via the six-kilometre boat ride from his lodge—to visit one of his neighbours, a trapper I happened to be staying with. Cutting the motor on his boat, the young American jumped on the dock and made his way up to the trapper's log cabin.

He had just arrived from his winter sojourn at his carpenter's job back home in Boulder, Colorado, and was getting his camp ready for the summer opening and the arrival of his first guests. Like a kid with a new toy, the energetic fishing camp operator beamed his happiness at being back in the surroundings he says are about as close to paradise as he's going to get—at least in this lifetime.

"I just love it up here. I mean, where better could you spend your life if you had the freedom to choose?" he said, waving an arm around towards the lake and the surrounding spruce and jackpine forest that's his summer home.

Four years ago he first set his eyes on the lake, another American tourist enjoying the good fishing in northern Saskatchewan. The fishing was good, the scenery spectacular, the tranquility awesome, and coincidentally the lake carried the same Foster name, so why not ask the camp owner if the place was for sale? It was mere whim that caused his query, but when the proprietor said that the place was indeed up for sale, Foster had to swallow hard.

"I'd asked him more to fill in time than anything else. When I realized I could actually own the camp, I forgot about the fishing and thought only of ways I could bring the purchase off."

Fishing trip over, he arrived home in Colorado and immediately dragged his father back to Saskatchewan to find out his opinion on the project. By this time, Foster had somewhat cooled to the idea, worried about the practicality of running a business he knew little about. However, his father provided new enthusiasm.

"He told me that if I didn't go for the deal I'd end up kicking my butt for the rest of my life," Foster said, smiling at the memory.

For a while it looked as if his Canadian dream would have to be put on hold. The bankers he met with told him they were not really thrilled about lending $100,000 for a Saskatchewan fishing camp. When all looked lost, a private investor came up with the necessary cash.

So at 24, one of the youngest, if not *the* youngest northern outfitter in the province, Foster set about attracting clients to his new camp. Attending sports shows around the U.S., and talking a mile a minute to potential customers about the terrific fishing in the area, Foster started building up his clientele.

Despite his lack of knowledge on operating a fishing camp, he knew he had a lot going for him in his new venture. An experienced carpenter, mechanic, and cook, Foster realized he had many of the bases covered as far as running a successful camp was concerned.

And in a very competitive industry he's starting to shine. Last year he had 54 tourists stay at Koo Sto; this year he hopes for as many as 100. Virtually all his customers are American, and that's where Foster concentrates his advertising and publicity efforts.

It's hard work, but that's something this fellow is not afraid of. All the cash acquired from his construction work is ploughed back into the Saskatchewan project, and while he has a few more years to pay off his loan, he's confident he'll make it.

"I'll pay it off okay," he says emphatically. "I have a lot of incentive to make this thing work. Every time I pound a nail into a piece of wood I think of this place. On a noisy construction site I can just close my eyes for a second and imagine myself back here. You just hold your breath, and everything is so still, so silent, you wonder if the world has stopped turning."

Frank Sudol in his log home near Paddockwood.

Teacher Branched Out
to Follow His Dreams

I suppose the best present anyone could put under our Christmas tree is a brightly wrapped package containing an answer to our dreams. We all have dreams—of places we'd rather be, of things we'd rather be doing—and at Christmas they bubble more towards the surface of our conscious thoughts.

Well, Frank Sudol also had dreams, found his life in conflict with those dreams, and decided that life was too short to be messing around with things that weren't fun. That decision led to him quitting his 17-year career as a high school biology teacher in Alberta, and spending his "nest egg" money over the next six years travelling and seeing a world he had only previously read about.

He was in his early 40s when he opted out of doing things he didn't want to do. Now at 60, his travelling days are done; he went when the going was good, he says, and now he's found his home.

Today he grows Christmas trees, and is one of the founders and first president of the growers' provincial association. He's also a fast-rising star in the wood turning business, making exquisite and delicate bowls, vases, and chalices from the birch that grows just beyond his yard. Ironically, he lives on the old family homestead, a small farm near Paddockwood, north of Prince Albert. It was a place he couldn't wait to leave as he was growing up.

"I hated it. We were dirt poor. I think we had one old beat-up crescent wrench between us, and I was the one who kept being blamed if it couldn't be found."

So Frank left, choosing an education track that would leave him with a couple of degrees, in education and biology, and an urge to teach. That worked for a while, but he figures he taught for too long.

"Not too many people should teach high school longer than three years," he smiles.

However, it was good experience and there are many great memories from those years. Besides, he says everything he's learned in botany and biology he's putting to good use nowadays on his Christmas tree farm.

"When I moved here in 1975 I wanted to prove I could make a living off a quarter-section of land, and I used my knowledge of trees to do just that."

He grows Scots pine, balsam fir, and white spruce, breeding and cross-pollinating trees to produce specimens that grow best in our climate and soil. In his workshop he produces some spectacular artistic pieces "made from the rough old birch tree" that sell for more than $300 each. This end of his enterprise is becoming increasingly profitable, with his artwork soon to appear in New York and Los Angeles.

Both careers—his trees and his art—allow him to live where he loves, on the land and near his friends. Here he looks life straight in the face, and both Frank and the globe seem to be smiling at each other. He's discovered what we all should know, that we make our own choices in life.

"The point is to make good choices, choices that suit us as individuals, and be ready to change and adapt to changing circumstances when they hit us," he told me, as we sat sipping coffee inside the massive log house he and his partner, Lois Laycraft, built together.

Virtually all the work on the house was done by the couple. The giant logs that make up the house's construction are white spruce, cut from the forest of trees on the farm. Frank also took plumbing and electrical courses to gather enough confidence to install the plumbing and wiring in his new home.

"I wasn't skilled in these areas so I became skilled. I adapted to my needs, if you like," he says.

Many folks have an inner terror of change and see it as a threat rather than an opportunity, Frank claims.

"Nothing stays the same and that's okay. Listen, there are a thousand million ideas floating around in the ether," he says, pointing a hand vigorously towards the heavens. "You just need to pick one out and run with it."

He's a man of strong convictions, someone who shoots his opinions from the hip. On topics from forestry conservation and soil ecology to the crucial need of farm diversification he's become a popular after-dinner speaker in agricultural circles.

"People say, 'That's good for you, but I couldn't do that, I'm no artist.' But I tell them that a few years ago neither was I."

He's a walking, talking example of a farm diversification success story, but he has a bottom line for anyone pursuing a dream. Stay out of debt, he says, and move away from thoughts of security.

"If you're in debt others will control your destiny. If you dwell on being secure you'll kill your natural ability to connect with the billion ideas that are waiting for you to pick up out of the ether."

Baldwin Malec reflects on 25 years of New Year's dances.

There's a Butterfly
on My Dance Card

Ah yes, New Year's dances, the stuff of Saskatchewan memories. The pop of Baby Duck corks, noisemakers exploding in your ears, wet kisses from total strangers, and—in Saskatchewan—music by the Cottonpickers.

I recall one particular New Year's dance when the group was playing to a full house at the Manhattan, just east of Saskatoon. I arrived a few minutes before midnight, having spent too long at a house party in the city. I couldn't get past the Hatt's foyer and spent the first part of that New Year thawing out my dance cleats.

This week, I met up with sax player and clarinetist Baldwin Malec, who shared some of the 25 years of memories of New Year's festivities and other dances he played as a member of the renowned Cottonpickers.

"I loved every minute of my musical life," says Baldwin, a retired high school teacher in Prince Albert. "They were the good old days, when old-style music, the music you could dance to, was king."

Growing up on the farm, Baldwin had little contact with music, except for the luck of having a talented mom with a fine singing voice. As a boy Baldwin also developed his singing ability, but it wasn't until he was in his early 20s that he learned to play musical instruments.

He was a latecomer to the musical scene, but he was a natural. Baldwin learned to play by ear, and there wasn't a tune he couldn't put together. He was invited to join the fledgling Cottonpickers in 1960.

"It was a great time. There can't be anything better in life than being allowed to do what you do best, and I really liked my music," Baldwin says.

But music was only one component of being a Cottonpicker. As a member of the audience, the toughest part was forking out the 10 bucks or so to get in to the hall. For the group the easy part was playing; getting there was the tricky bit. Transportation logistics were not easily overcome in rural Saskatchewan.

"We started with an old trailer towed behind the car, but that didn't last long. Then we bought a used Saskatoon Transit bus, which could never pass 55 mph—way too slow, so we ended up replacing it with an STC highway bus."

He remembers one trip to Yorkton, when the bus started to use oil in a big way.

"We'd go 20 miles and have to put in a quart, then 15 miles and put in another quart. Finally we stopped at a garage and they sold us a 45-gallon drum of waste oil, and that got us through."

There were impassable roads, nail biting times on small chartered planes, and vehicle breakdowns to cope with, but the group never missed a venue, says Baldwin.

"There were times we came awfully close, but we were professionals and all we could think about were the disappointed folks waiting to dance."

There's no doubt Baldwin's teaching career came first. While dedicated to his students, he found music a great relief from the stress of school bureaucracy. But his full-time high school career and his hectic Cottonpickers schedule did cause a few problems on the domestic front.

"Like the time my wife, Irene, got mad at me leaving for a dance one weekend. She took all my white shirts and threw them in the muddy garden," he laughs. "She did rewash them for me, though," he adds.

Although he left the group in 1984, Baldwin says the Cottonpickers are still very much in evidence on stages across the province and are still led by the group's founder, Lew Bell.

"Lew deserves a lot of credit for keeping us in line. It wasn't easy holding that many fragile egos together when we were on the road."

Baldwin still plays, these days with a group called Night Fire. But his dance schedule is much reduced nowadays because most events can't afford live music, he says.

"There's not a lot of call for live music. Maybe it's too expensive and maybe people's tastes have changed."

That's too bad. The romantic atmosphere surrounding the dance hall, the air of expectation, and the excitement made weekends all too short. Under the afterglow of freshly Brylcreemed hair, it was a place to meet girls and demonstrate the effectiveness of the very latest in aftershave.

Like most things in life, New Year's Eve dances are much more fun when you're young and all your body parts are still intact. Of course it's probably all of youth's excessive activities, such as New Year's Eve parties, that lead to the general decay and demobilization of our human frames. But, for me, it's enough just to have memories of those rip-roaring year-end extravaganzas; when the world was young, the schottische and butterfly were king, and fast-moving feet went in roughly the right direction.

Aurore Grosjean admires the weather vanes made by her husband, Clem.

Prairie Wind
——— Stirs Up Memories ———

Probably anyone who has reached mid-life has lost a loved one. That's one of living's tough parts, but obviously unavoidable in our own often-lonely journey to that distant horizon. Luckily, we have our memories, our scrapbooks, our photo albums, and our thoughts.

Remembering the person with affection and love—the smiles, the tears, and all the lessons we learned through knowing her or him—somehow keeps that person alive in spirit. That makes our own life more meaningful.

It only takes the stirring of the prairie wind to bring those good memories alive for Aurore Grosjean. In her garden at the edge of Cut Knife, a small community 50 kilometres west of the Battlefords, Aurore is surrounded by memories of her husband.

Clem Grosjean died almost eight years ago, but the ploughs, carts, and figures that he crafted into weather vanes still catch the strong prairie winds from their perches in the family garden. Aurore, 80, never has to look far to find out where the wind is blowing.

"He loved making these things," she explains, showing her visitor around her flower garden, where the intricate wind pointers live.

Over the years, many others have enjoyed the sight of Clem's colourful creations.

"People from everywhere were always stopping to take pictures of Clem's work," she says.

Aurore says her husband, a farmer, was a real worker and was never happy unless he was making "this or that." Bad health forced an early retirement from the family farm, and the couple moved into Cut Knife in 1974.

"He still needed to work at something, and making crafts and other stuff made him happy. Some of his work is now in the local museum, but I like to keep these around. They were important to him."

So as she prunes and plants, waters and weeds her garden, she's kept company by the whistle of the wind turbine or the slow creaking of weather vanes as the wind takes a change. It is strange how the most poignant reminders of loved ones are not so much contained in the photographs we keep around, but in the items and things touched or fashioned by these precious people.

For the rest of us it might be an old pipe, a pair of slippers, a sweater still hanging in the closet; somehow all these things can become the stuff of memories, providing the visual jolts that take us back. The external images we match up with the pictures in our minds are much more powerful than the ones Kodak physically cements for us in perpetuity.

As our days pass, more of our friends and family will follow that path into death, emphasizing our vulnerability to our own inevitable fate. That thought prompts my curiosity as to what my loved ones might hold on to in my memory.

There won't be any monuments, that's for sure. I'm hopeless at building things. I don't smoke, so the pipe is not an item to be reckoned with. I generally lose any carpet slippers that I'm given as gifts, and my old sweaters end their days lining the cat's basket.

Still, looking around the fascinating creations that Clem Grosjean left behind, and considering how much pleasure they have brought to others, it makes you think about these things.

Walter Buller: hunter of gold.

The Man Who Moils for Gold

Think of a couple of million hectares of shag carpet and drop a needle, then hire someone to hunt it down. By the way, it helps if the needle is solid gold.

That's one way of looking at problems facing prospectors in Saskatchewan's north as they examine and chip rock surfaces in their quest for wealth. With billions of dollars worth of potential ore bodies waiting to be uncovered, these tough men fan out across the northern landscape in hot pursuit.

The word "prospector" evokes its own images: the Klondike, Eldorado, gold, uranium, the motherlode, the tingling feelings of frontier life, unfathomable wealth ... that's how many of us imagine the prospector in his battle of discovery. He's often seen as a hero, a rugged individual defying the odds Mother Nature throws his way, with sand in his teeth and only a mule for company.

Maybe we admire prospectors because of their tough struggle. Climbing mountains, crossing deserts, and fighting the elements before the final victory satisfies a certain ethic of suffering before deliverance. But it's a scene safely romanticized from the plush couch and the warmth of the television. Reality is quite different ...

Behind his bushy beard and a personality as broad as the Precambrian Shield, Walter Buller hides the instincts of a hunter—a hunter of gold.

His friends claim the prospector has the Midas touch when it comes to discovering gold and other valuable mineral deposits in the wilderness of northern Saskatchewan. They point to the half-dozen or so commercial-sized ore deposits he's found over the years and say, in hushed voices, that he can smell gold. One long-time associate lists Buller's ore body discoveries with the delight of Casanova describing his conquests.

The prospector cuts a fascinating figure and is a mine of information about the old days of prospecting. Between sips from a coffee-blackened cup, Buller quietly talks about this copper find, or that lead-zinc property, or the big gold deposit he uncovered a few years ago.

His is a story of almost 40 years of prospecting in Canada's north; almost a lifetime of playing detective with Mother Nature. As prospecting goes, Buller is to mineral deposits what Arnold Palmer is to fairways. Buller's playing area, however, is a million hectares of wilderness. His silent landscape is made up of trees, lakes, and muskeg, his audience the cheers thousands of kilometres away on the stock exchange floors of Toronto and Vancouver.

Millions change hands every year as mining companies, brokers, stock promoters, and investors gaze at electronic ticker tapes bringing them the news that could start with a few rock chips produced by a prospector's hammer.

But there's no sign of such wealth in Buller's tiny trailer, settled firmly in this community 450 kilometres north of Saskatoon. There's no Cadillac outside and there's no cigar jutting out of his mouth. Instead, a moist tailor-made is anchored to his lip as if it grew there.

A sugar-filled Vogue tobacco can is as close to silverware as Buller's table is likely to display.

He's a larger than life personality, a rough, tough individual, the picture of a hero straight out of a scene from *Treasure of the Sierra Madre*. Buller seems more John Huston than the real thing, except this 57-year-old didn't need Hollywood to create his character.

He says he was 18 and verging on juvenile delinquency when he left British Columbia for northern Saskatchewan in search of his fortune. It was 1952, a time when Saskatchewan's north was beginning to receive increasing attention from the mining community. The glamour of working a stake and the dreams of nuggets of gold and trainloads of copper led him north to join an exploration crew.

He had started out from Abbotsford with $500 in hard-earned cash. By the time his plane landed at remote Camsell Portage, he was down to $50 and a half-bottle of rum. It was the last plane in before freeze-up and there was no turning back.

"The men there gave me hell ... told me I should have brought $50 worth of rum if I planned on staying."

All that winter of 1952 he stayed in a frost-coated tent working in a uranium mine waiting for spring and the prospecting season to begin.

Searching the wilderness for minerals had been Buller's dream since childhood. "I used to get hell because my pockets were always full of rocks by the time I got home from school," he says.

That first summer in the bush accompanied by blackflies, mosquitoes, and loneliness was a season of disappointment. But it also introduced him to the reality of a prospector's life.

"You find out pretty quick that promising finds are few and far between, but you never really get used to the disappointment."

But if the disappointment is hard to take, the few—very few—times the hammer reveals sufficient traces of valuable minerals bring joy that's hard to describe. He slaps his chest and his gleaming eyes widen.

"It gets you here. It feels like your chest is going to pound apart."

For a number of years Buller searched the bush and learned from the old-timers skills that can't be taught from books. He was away from civilization for as long as six months at a time. Sometimes alone, sometimes with partners, he peeled back moss, scratched rock surfaces and chiseled at boulders, looking for the tell-tale signs of minerals. The quest was for the green-blue tinge of copper, the orange of zinc and lead, and, of course, the king of metals, the yellow gleam of gold.

Normally, Buller would work for a mining company or an exploration outfit that would pay him a wage and pick up his expenses. One year in the late '50s he went freelance, deciding to go it alone without sponsorship.

"Ended belly-up. Flat broke. I had to find work down south to pay for my grubstake."

He was back in the bush the following year, grubstaked by an exploration contractor. Somewhere about 150 kilometres out of La Ronge he found a rock with streaks of gold-bearing pyrite running through it.

Crushing the rock and burning off the residue produced two things. First came the tiny tail of yellow material at the end of the waste: gold. This was instantly followed by the pounding in Buller's chest.

Now prospecting is a cloak-and-dagger operation. A prospector almost works by the same rules as a CIA agent. But his first loyalty is to the mining company that hired him. It's still a business where a handshake seals a contract, and Buller takes that trust seriously.

When the company plane brings supplies, it takes the newly discovered samples and a detailed prospector's report back to head office. After careful analysis and further investigation, boardroom decisions set development plans in motion if warranted. This rarely means a mine, however. More likely, Buller explains, the company will sit on the find until it's profitable to extract the minerals. Profitability is determined by the remoteness of the find, size of the ore body, market price, and the cost of extraction.

However, the company's stock is where the action is. A promising discovery can send share prices through the roof, hence the secrecy, says Buller, touching the side of his nose with a knowing finger.

"The problem for me is, I'm stuck in the bush while all this hubbub is going on. I find the stuff but can't get in on the action."

What he can expect as a prospector, depending on the deal made with the company that hires him, is $150 to $200 a day plus his expenses—his grubstake. The company flies him in and out and brings his supplies. For five months during the summer, Buller will examine particularly interesting sites and stake claims for the company if anything promising turns up.

Promising discoveries also mean extra money in the form of bonuses, he says. "One year I made an extra $18,000 in bonus money."

In the winter he makes the trip out to British Columbia and the house trailer that is home. Sometimes he does some prospecting there, though more often he uses the time to spend his earnings from Saskatchewan. By spring, he says, he's itching to get back to the north and begin again looking for Eldorados. He says life in the wilderness agrees with him.

While he's swamped a canoe, had his tent ripped by bears a couple of times, and had a close call with a charging bull moose, the life of a northern prospector is unbeatable.

"Heck, where are you safe? I've had my mobile home broken into five times, and that's by people."

Maybe it's the call of the wild rather than the scream of gold that takes him north every year, Buller speculates. But somewhere out there is a genuine motherlode, he says. It has to be. And that's a powerful hook for any prospector. It's the only way he'll ever get rich, he says, a smile parting his beard.

"I'm on my second million. I gave up on the first."

Buller takes a few books on his tour of duty into the bush. But between working, eating, and sleeping, most days are pretty full. He says there are a billion stars to look at, though, and that's adequate compensation.

"I've had two heart attacks in the bush. You know, your pulse stops and you feel your chest is blowing up, and there's no gold in sight. That's when you know it's a heart attack."

But the work gets in his blood, he says. So every summer he makes it back to Saskatchewan's north and takes another chance at finding the big one. You never know, he says.

He's a loner. He never married. Buller sometimes looks around and sees young kids, and sometimes figures he's missed out on something a long time ago. But we all pick our own road to travel, he says.

Frank Miller with his latest replica of the **Northcote.**

Historic Steamer
Gets New Berth

C lose your eyes for a moment and really see; it's the best way to bring history alive. That's what Frank Miller did one Sunday afternoon in 1955 while he listened to a radio program focusing on the only naval battle ever to take place on the prairies.

Imagine for a minute that you are on the steamboat *Northcote*: guns firing from all directions, the racket of splintering wood as bullets shatter into guard rails, and the screams of friends around you not lucky enough to dodge Louis Riel's soldiers' withering fire.

That afternoon Frank turned up the radio's volume and, closing his eyes, was transported back to 1885 when events of the Northwest

Rebellion were unfolding in dramatic fashion. Battles and killings at Duck Lake, Frog Lake, and Fish Creek had taken place and General Middleton's soldiers were closing in to fight Riel at Batoche.

The steamer *Northcote*, a boat used to transport settlers and salesmen along prairie waterways, found itself commandeered as a man-of-war. Loaded with soldiers and ammunition, it made its way from Saskatchewan Landing slowly down the South Saskatchewan River towards Batoche.

Heavy firing by rebel sharpshooters prevented the *Northcote* from making it to Batoche. Complicating matters further, a ferry cable, strung across the river and timely hoisted by the rebels, damaged the boat's smokestacks and wheelhouse. The *Northcote* withdrew under heavy fire and, while not playing a role in any more fighting for Batoche, did carry wounded back to Saskatoon.

When the radio broadcast ended, and Frank once again opened his eyes, he wanted to pass on a little of that history to others. He wanted to do his part in preserving the province's brief moment in naval history. The fact that he had been born in Aberdeen, only a scant 40 kilometres from the scene of the fighting, gave his project added meaning.

"I knew I had to build a replica of the *Northcote*. It was my way of helping hold on to our past," Frank told me when I visited his home in North Battleford.

Thirty-six years ago, the retired accountant followed through on the promise to himself and built his boat. It wasn't easy. Even after extensive research, to help build up a picture of the ship in his mind, the only dimension of the boat he knew was its length, 150 feet.

However, despite the fact that he had only a single archival photograph of the boat to work from, the construction work was a success. The metre-long replica of the *Northcote* currently sits in Moose Jaw's Western Development Museum. A second version of the steam ship, built by Frank under contract to Parks Canada in 1961, found a berth at the museum in Batoche.

He's just finished his third version of the famous craft. Lately, more extensive research had unearthed several more pictures of the boat, so his working knowledge was more precise for his most recent version. After spending 200 working hours on the construction of this latest beauty, it's ready to be launched towards its destination, a new museum in Cumberland House.

"It's appropriate that it should be there. The real *Northcote* ended its days being beached on the shores of that community the year after the rebellion."

Around the turn of the century, residents of Cumberland House, concerned about the safety hazards presented by the rotting vessel, decided to burn the hulk. While the town no longer has the real thing, they hired Frank last year to provide a replica to help fire up the community's imagination about that critical time in Saskatchewan's history.

As for the builder, turning the pages of history books is always a little easier when you have an accurate image of events floating in your mind, and his *Northcote* replica provides that. There were also other rewards.

"I found it kind of therapeutic to get down to the fine work needed on the boat. It was no chore to put down my ledgers and pick up a tiny drill or knife to do some boat work."

Personally, I'm not much good at model building, but I find history to be very therapeutic. I took a good long look at Frank's latest *Northcote* stern-wheeler, and closed my eyes ...

"I grew up on a farm. There were three of us girls, no boys; we were the boys, and we sure worked. I don't remember learning to walk, but I remember picking stones."

The Secret of Longevity Is So Incredibly Simple

There's something about living in a small town that's got to be good for your longevity. It must have something to do with the ample supply of fresh air with which rural residents stoke up their old lungs. Maybe it's because there are fewer folks around, and fewer cars, trucks, and buses dotting the landscape, so there's substantially less body-damaging stress permeating the systems of rural retirees.

"You sit yourself down and don't mind that I'm missing my soaps. It's not going to kill me to ignore one episode," Alice Walton says, taking a last look at the uncoiling love tryst playing out on the TV set before turning a switch and toppling the anguished drama into temporary black oblivion.

Alice lives in Rabbit Lake, a tiny community about 85 kilometres northeast of The Battlefords, and as a vibrant 83-year-old, she's certainly a sound representative for my rural longevity theory.

"Of course that doesn't mean to say I'm going to be around this time next year, not the way people seem to be dropping off nowadays. Life is unpredictable, very uncertain. Would you like a cup of coffee?"

Statistics seem to indicate that having a pet improves the quality of life for seniors. While Alice is definitely a lover of animals, she walks that thin line of all cat lovers who also enjoy feeding birds.

"I've always had cats; they are lovely animals, but as you can see I like to encourage birds around my house," she explains, pointing through the window of her small home, to the lineup of bird houses in her back yard; a veritable suburban free fly-zone. "Since my last cat died I've decided no more cats."

Keeping active is a major component in staying both physically and emotionally well. Alice has had lots of practice.

"I grew up on a farm. There were three of us girls, no boys. We were the boys, and we sure worked. I don't remember learning to walk, but I remember picking stones. These were my stone pickers," she says, holding out two hands for me to inspect. "Every year I'd pick stones and every year there'd be a new crop of them."

Talking about the old days called for some visual aids to memory, so Alice brought out a stack of photo albums and scanned the black and white images that returned her to childhood. Horses, threshing machines, binders, wood piles, barns, more horses: silent reflections of a personal journey through life in rural Saskatchewan.

After their father died, the three sisters continued to operate the farm. For 20 years, until it was finally sold in 1972, they raised cattle and grew grain as they had always done.

"But enough was enough; I decided that I'd had enough of life on the farm so I walked into town and bought this place," Alice says cheerfully.

For the first two years she busied herself altering the house—knocking old walls down, putting new walls up, and installing a bathroom addition to her home.

"I'm an old maid," she laughs, eyes sparkling, "so I did most of the work myself. I did need some help with the rafters on the addition; you can't do that by yourself."

She has no driving licence, doesn't believe in credit cards, and doesn't owe a cent.

"I still prefer using my wood cookstove; it has a real good oven ... I don't bake bread anymore; the last batch turned out like lead. But chopping wood is no hardship. The fact is I find chopping wood to be real enjoyable. That's my problem, though, I end up cutting the wood too small and it burns too fast so I have to stop myself."

While she's happy at home, she's also interested in the world around her. "I'm a traveller, I am," she says, reaching for another photo album. "I've been lots of places. I visited England and I've been to Hawaii. I love Hawaii. If I could convince a friend to go with me, I would be off again. It's no fun travelling alone."

Judging by the Christmas cards, still suspended on a string around her living-room window, she has no shortage of friends. Around town and the district Alice visits with them, sharing coffee times and playing the odd game of cards. Wednesday afternoons, she walks over to the nursing home to play bingo and, if there's time, a round of kaiser.

"But I do like to get home for 'Wheel of Fortune' if I can."

Not that Alice watches a lot of television; it cuts into her reading time. She especially likes to peruse her Bible, as well as the occasional Harlequin romance.

"I try to read a couple of chapters of the Bible a day. I find it's like food to me; I can't live without it. I'm going through it for the fourth time."

Enthusiasm. That's what a long life needs, and Alice seems charged with it. She's no materialist, but she confesses to being attached to her collection of salt and pepper shakers, a hobby she's had for the past 20 years or so. They come in all shapes and sizes. Alsatians, miniature ketchup bottles, Las Vegas gambling machines, matching French poodles, twin grenadier guardsmen ... the pairs stand shoulder to shoulder, almost spilling out of glass display cases around her home.

"I got seven more sets for Christmas. That brings me up to, let me see," she says, examining a page of penciled notes. "It's 771 at last count. This isn't a hobby anymore, it's a disease."

Alice smiles.

If it is a disease, then collecting salt and pepper shakers must be another integral component of living a long, full life.

Greg Hoenmans and his dog, Rifle, are ready for a bike ride.

The Master
of Penny-pinching

I've never met anyone who has made such an art out of watching his pennies as Greg Hoenmans. In our consumer-crazed world, where spending money has almost a ring of religious fervour, Greg can stretch his paycheque as if it were a demonstration of Hooke's law of elasticity. The Saskatoon maintenance worker has developed his common-sense frugality to a fine art.

While the majority of the western world can't wait to be separated from their hard-earned shekels, Greg has recognized the value of his bucks, and works just as hard to keep a tight grip on them. He certainly didn't buy into the rules of a consumer society, where the credit card has become the compass used to navigate the unsuspecting into economic cul-de-sacs.

Luckily the 41-year-old has the survival skills to travel under his own sails. That's largely because he possesses a penchant for invention, combined with a keen streak of common sense, that allows him to avoid the usual merchandizing traps the rest of us fall into. The end result is a huge saving in cash.

Take for instance Greg's latest gizmo, the pet trailer he pulls behind his mountain bike. He uses the neat home-made buggy to transport his border-collie/terrier around town. His dog, Rifle, enjoys these excursions in the trailer so much that the sight of man and dog travelling around together hardly causes an extra glance in the neighbourhood nowadays.

He could have faced a bill of up to $400 if he had purchased a commercially manufactured bike trailer, but that's not Greg's way of operating. Instead, he visited a few salvage yards that he frequents from time to time in and around the city. He began to come up with ideas on how he could put together a cheap bike-buggy.

"I picked up a couple of wheels at an automotive salvage. I paid about $20 for both of them. I got an extra wheel, just for the axle, at a scrap iron place, and my wife bought me the tires," Greg told me.

After a visit to a local bike shop, where he "snooped some ideas," Greg perfected a knuckle spring system that would allow the trailer hitch to bend when the bike turned a corner. A 10-gallon plastic jug— cut in half—formed the actual carrying basket for Rifle.

"Funny name to call a dog, Rifle, but I got him from the SPCA and it was the only masculine name I could come up with when I had him fixed. I felt I owed him that at least," Greg informed me.

Since he assembled the first prototype in the spring, he has had to make a few design alterations to make the machine more functional.

"I think I have it working fine right now. Maybe I should patent some parts of this. Some of the construction is pretty original."

His bike trailer is a very visible reflection of Greg's ingenuity; however, his money-saving do-it-yourself skills are not always focused on his pet dog.

"My wife and I went camping in the States and found all the campgrounds had these love swings. They are kind of like regular swings, but on these types there's room for two people. Well, I looked at them closely and figured out I could make one myself, so when we got back that's what I did."

The swings in the campgrounds were made of wood. Greg wanted something a little stronger so he made his love seat out of steel. Looking at it you'd imagine it could survive a thousand years of serious swinging.

Of course, it's not only money-saving that keeps him focused on work projects. He loves the challenge of fixing stuff. From household problems to auto mechanics, Greg can swing a hammer or handle a screwdriver sufficiently well to do many jobs himself.

Build himself a boat trailer? No problem. Replace the rusting bucket of his wheelbarrow? All that project needed was an oil drum and a cutting torch and he was back in business.

"I work shift work and get four days off some weeks, so I'd go crazy if I didn't give myself some tasks to do. All this keeps me out of trouble. I'm too busy to spend money. Maybe that's the trick," he laughs.

Vic Prytula probably has what you are looking for.

Small Country Store
Keeps Customers Happy

Somewhere between the candy display and the bullet-shaped cigarette lighters Victor Prytula found what his customer was looking for—a pot repair package.

"Not much call for these anymore, and not too many places stock
them, but I do," said the 64-year-old Prytula, a small note of triumph
in his voice.

His customer, a farmer, seemed happy at this discovery and examined the small package.

"So you must be enjoying the rain?" the store keeper asked by way
of small talk.

The local farmer glanced out of the doorway at the mud-spattered vehicle sitting in the street.

"Jeez, we hardly had any. What we had dried before it hit the ground," he said dispassionately.

For almost eight decades Prytula's general store has served this tiny community about 120 kilometres northeast of Saskatoon. From cans of beans to cultivator shovels, the family-owned store has passed a wide variety of merchandise across its counter.

Keeping his customers happy is what has kept his country store in operation, says Prytula, as he runs a hand through his thick grey hair. By maintaining a large inventory, he keeps choices open to a wide cross-section of customers' whims and preferences.

"You never know what people are going to want when they come through that door. All you do know is that if you don't have it you can just about guarantee that's what they will want."

Prytula has done his best to prevent that problem. The result is what Madison Avenue might call intensive marketing. For the small store, with its packed display cases and crowded aisles, it means there isn't room to swing a cat.

But it's easy to get your choice of belts and suspenders, shirts and shorts, anniversary cups and bowls, or a good hickory-handled axe, Johnny Cash LPs, souvenir spoons, cookbooks. Even an "as seen on TV" $29.95 mini-sewing machine is available.

It might not be IBM or Westinghouse, but Prytula's store has survived the Great Depression, numerous booms and busts, and changing buying patterns and still managed to keep the doors open and turn a profit.

Since Vic's father, John, started the store back in 1915, rural Saskatchewan has seen great social upheaval, most of its farm-based population moving to more urban settings for jobs. Tway didn't escape that phenomenon. With a population hovering around 25, Prytula's store can thank its still-loyal local customers plus the tourist trade that visits nearby Wakaw Lake.

Prytula lives just a few doors down from his store. Since his wife died in 1985 he has operated his business alone. But he thrives on the work. He's certainly used to it, having laboured in the old building since he left school.

His store is open five days a week, although he says summer is much busier than winter when both tourists and farmers ring the chimes on his cash register. It's not only regular consumer goods that people seek out in his store, he explains. There are antiques, merchandise left over from his father's days, that are increasingly in demand as customers recognize their value.

A five-cent pack of razor blades now sells for more than $2. Tokens from the meat rationing days of the Second World War go for a cool 50 cents a piece. A one-ounce package of Old Chum tobacco which sold in 1943 for 12 cents can be yours today, but you'll measure the cost in dollars.

There's something about a country store that captures the imagination for many of us, but operating one can quickly take away the glamour. Prytula thinks about this quite a bit when it comes to imagining what the future holds.

"I suppose at some point I won't be able to put in a full day and I'll have to retire. Can't tell you when that will be, though; I'm still enjoying myself."

Sister Callista Arnold listens to her friends' stories.

Nun Embraces
AIDS Victims

Through the hour-long visit, Sister Callista Arnold gently stroked Brent's hand. She had hugged him when she first came through his door, and then handed over the large pie dish she had brought with her. The hugging part of the visit is a ritual for Callista, who specializes in delivering warmth, and the occasional apple crumble, to the homes of friends such as Brent. Most of all, she brings love.

The Ursuline sister works at St. Anne's Parish, in the northern part of Saskatoon. She's responsible for the hospitality program run by her church: welcoming new members of the congregation, organizing volunteers to visit families in the community, and helping co-ordinate parish activities.

But this was her day off; she was visiting one of her friends with AIDS. For the past seven years, the 69-year-old Catholic sister has worked, laughed, and cried alongside the people of Saskatoon who live with HIV or full-blown AIDS. While her regular job with the church can get pretty hectic, she has made time to develop friendships with the ones she calls the invisible people.

"Most of society, I think, has rejected and ostracised these people and tries hard to ignore their existence," she says.

Callista does not. She embraces them, an intimate involvement that has been supported by her bishop and her congregation. There have been more than 40 of these friends listed in her address book, but some of these she no longer visits. These 10 are the ones who have died. Some of them have died in her arms, lost to the mysterious virus, lost to their families, and lost to the world.

Loss is something people with AIDS deal with all the time, Brent tells Sister Callista. Brent, 34, is gay. He lost his lover late last year—another victim of AIDS. The grief still drifts through his home.

"Since AIDS, it seems I have spent my time tallying losses: my friends who have died from it, my job, my car, my RRSPs. Sometimes it seems there's not much more to lose," he says softly.

Brent suffers from lengthy periods of desperate fatigue and severe muscle pain, which makes sustaining a job difficult. That means he has to rely on social assistance to help meet his expenses. But Brent says he's certainly not someone who would allow depression to swallow him up. He lives a full and active life, playing a major role in both local and national AIDS support groups.

Brent's cat strolls around the comfortable living room, checking out a warm shaft of early afternoon sunlight as a possible nap zone. Smoke, from a cigarette smouldering in the ashtray on the low coffee table, floats up towards the framed photographs of family and friends that line the walls. Callista continues to stroke Brent's hand.

"I think most of us look on the expressions HIV-positive and AIDS with a mixture of dread and relief. The dread comes from the reality of the awful prognosis for many of its sufferers; the relief arises out of the supposed reality that if we're not homosexual we are somehow immune from it," she says.

As increasing numbers of the heterosexual community are being diagnosed HIV-positive, it's time to move out of the darkness of denial that surrounds AIDS, Callista says. Whoever is being infected—gay or straight—they are human beings with ticking hearts and thinking minds; not flat, grey statistics we can file away and forget.

While the people with AIDS try to live their lives courageously, beyond the time bomb in their system, the connection with the virus extends far beyond their own bodies. These people have what we all have: families, friends, colleagues. All these people are affected by AIDS, Callista says.

John Eberts and his Belgian horses keep part of Saskatchewan's heritage alive.

Farmer Indulges His Love
of Heavy Horses

S houlder to shoulder, Tom and Jerry emerged from their stable, barely squeezing through the open barn door. General and Lee came next, bunching up close to make the same passage into daylight and joining the two bigger horses outside. At about 726 kilograms each, the two younger Belgian horses were smaller than Tom and Jerry by 181 or so kilograms.

"The two big 'uns weigh in around a tonne apiece," the owner of the four horses proudly told me.

John Eberts' horses reflect the pride of their owner. That's as it should be. But while the animals are tamed now, trained to do battle with plough and seeder, their passive bearing hides another heritage. These beasts are direct descendants of medieval battle horses bred in the Low Countries centuries ago.

Eberts has been around draft horses since he was a boy, when Saskatchewan farm production ultimately depended on good horseflesh to cultivate, seed, and harvest the crops of the pioneers.

They were hard times, but good times, and horses were pretty reliable most of the time, Eberts says. There were no worn bearings, broken crankshafts, flat tires, and oil changes to worry about then. There were also other advantages.

"You had companionship in the field. They were almost human, you might say. You got to know your horses and their different personalities and temperaments," Eberts says, wrapping a thick powerful hand around his horses' reins.

Today, the big horsepower tractors leave their wide tire tracks across the dusty soil of Saskatchewan fields, but back then it was real horse power that pulled the heavy machinery through the fields. Horses proved indispensable in the early development of Saskatchewan agriculture and were still active on many prairie farms well into the 1940s.

Eberts was barely in his teens when he first struggled along through the summerfallow with a seed drill and four horses. He's 67 now, but the memories of the dust, the clanking of harness, and the snort of an impatient or tired horse are still strong.

"Oh, it's like yesterday. I even remember the old horses' names."

As the mid-point of the century approached, most farmers were switching from horses to tractors, and Eberts joined them. His love for horses was overshadowed by the need to stay in business. In order to keep your head above water, it was necessary to increase grain production, and that meant mechanization, he says.

"Horses were forgotten about, I guess. I was too busy trying to raise my family and put food on the table."

That changed as he grew older and more established, and could pass on the farm's reins, so to speak, to his children. Then he decided to get back into the horse world, raising a new stable of Belgians to compete in horse-pulls across the prairies.

Past most folks' official retirement age, Eberts has freed up some of his time by renting out the remaining land of his Lumsden-area farm to his son and neighbours.

"I'm more a hobby farmer now, so I can spend more time fooling around with my horses," he explains.

However, he maintains strong connections to both his horses and his land. He puts in 20 acres of oats every year, seeded and harvested by the very horses that will end up eating the crop they sow.

"That way they pay for their keep," he smiles up at his charges, who look back at him through wide, glassy eyes. Worth up to $5,000 each, Belgian draft horses command more than just respect from their owners.

But Eberts' horses bring a lot of happiness to many other people besides their owner. Children come by the busload from nearby schools to watch them in action, reconnecting with an almost forgotten piece of provincial history.

"That's the part I find most rewarding. It's keeping part of our heritage alive," he says.

The horses stand more than a foot taller than the stocky Eberts, but under his command are as docile as lambs. With their massive hooves, as wide as dinner plates, breaking through the soft earth, they stand waiting for orders. Not that there are a lot of orders these days; modern machinery sees to that.

"But when they get a chance they love to work, and there's no finer sight than to see them in action doing what they were bred to do," he says.

Dale Burechailo and her mother, Martha (left), regard the boulder
on which Dale has painted her impressions of pioneer life.

Field Stone
Reflects Family History

A bout 130 kilometres northeast of Saskatoon, near the small community of Domremy, a large rock at the edge of a field tells a story. Painted on the stone are bright, acrylic scenes from agricultural life that take you on a journey into the past.

The pictures reflect on the early days of European settlement— oxen, plough, threshing machine, hay wagon—and thundering combine and powerful grain truck complete the history lesson.

"And that thatched-roof home is just like the house my parents were raised in. That outdoor oven is the same as what my grandmother would have baked bread in," says the painter, her hand outstretched towards the contoured images.

Dale Burechailo looks up from the large boulder and across the snow-covered field that has been home to the rock for more than 30 years, since her father first pulled and tugged it out of the ground to erect it on the slope overlooking the approach to the family farm.

Dale is justly proud of the work that she and her friend and art instructor, Jiang Nan, completed late last year. It was painted on weekends and days off from her stressful job as an operating room nurse at Royal University Hospital. Dale and Nan worked from May until October before the final protective coat of clear varnish could be applied.

In some ways the finished painting came a little bit late. One regret for Dale is that her father was not around to witness what became of his rock. Mike Burechailo died last February.

"He knew I'd planned on painting a family history on the rock. He was anxious to see what it would look like," she says. "It's a big disappointment that he never had the chance."

But there are many other witnesses to the epic painting efforts of Dale and Nan. In fact, the rock has become somewhat of a tourist attraction in the area. The most important member of the appreciative audience, as far as Dale is concerned, is her mother.

I met her mom after we'd made the short drive from the rock's location to the Burechailo farm. Wrapped up from head to toe against the early morning winter cold, the elderly woman walked out of the frost-edged barn carrying a metal pail.

She turned to her daughter: "You take him inside and put some coffee on. I still have to finish milking the cow."

With that gentle command to Dale, Martha Burechailo scurried off to continue the neverending job of farm chores, while Dale and I followed her advice and escaped to the warmth of the house.

Martha is 78, but you would never know it. Closing in on her eighth decade she's still as lively and energetic as the day when she and her husband began their life together a half-century ago.

When she returned to her neat farm bungalow, Martha removed her boots, peeled off layers of winter clothing, and joined us for coffee.

"Mike was always talking about that rock, always wondering what Dale was going to paint on it," she says.

She and her husband had worked as a team on the farm. Growing grain, raising chickens, feeding cattle, milking cows: Martha had laboured long and hard alongside Mike to make a living during some pretty tough years.

Droughts and frosts, good crops and bad crops, feasts and famines;

the couple survived to raise their children and join the scattered farm community in social and religious occasions that were—and remain—part of traditional life in rural Saskatchewan. The couple lived through a fast-changing history, seeing the likes of Dolly and Queenie being replaced with John Deeres, as horses and oxen gave up to other, more powerful breeds of horsepower.

Dale captured these passing eras and experiences on her father's rock. The powerful juxtaposition of simplicity swept by technological changes—the times her parents had lived through—that was her inspiration.

Photo scrapbooks play a big part in helping families stay connected with their own histories. Dale, through her painted rock, has gone an important step further, illustrating the flow of her family's farm history into the very landscape where it all happened.

"I wanted the rock to become a monument in a way, a visual memory to the work and efforts of my parents. I think my dad would have approved of it. I know, while he's not here, he is seeing it. I'm sure of that," Dale smiles.

We returned to the site, to take a longer inspection of the rock permanently lodged in the quiet field. Surrounded by snow-silent countryside it was not difficult to understand Dale's confidence that, somewhere, fatherly eyes were looking approvingly at his daughter's work.

*Don O'Brien tends his flock with help
from hired hands Gem and Snuffy.*

Get Along,
Little Lambs

The clouds in the south were surging and cascading into aerial images of Niagara Falls—sometimes a Mont Blanc avalanche—as they buffeted and elbowed a timid blue sky into obscurity. This casualty of nature was not lost on Don O'Brien, cast out—along with his horse, two border collies, and at last count about 900 head of sheep—across a broad expanse of prairie.

A shepherd by trade, O'Brien watches his flock and the heavens with an almost biblical acuity.

"We're going to get something before the day's out."

He casts sunglassed eyes to the sky, as vivid stabs of lightning slash across the blue-black Wagnerian backdrop.

Gem and Snuffy, his four-legged hired hands, sit and pant next to the patient hooves of the big three-year-old paint that carries the shepherd around the enormous grazing areas of the Elbow-Willner PFRA pasture.

High in the saddle, O'Brien can survey the sheep and lambs that make up his flock. For about four months—from the middle of May until September—the genial shepherd will be responsible for the safety and security of his charges until the sheep are picked up by their owners and taken back to their own farms. With just the company of his horse, dogs, and the occasional Pecos Kid paperback, O'Brien watches and waits out the long days riding herd on his flock.

He rises at 5 to greet a working day that lasts until 7 or 8 at night. First thing after breakfast he will release the sheep from the pen, where they spend every night safe from marauding coyotes. For the rest of the day he follows them around their grazing range. While the flock might munch over a four- or five-kilometre radius from their central pen area, the sheep will often meander as many as 15 to 20 kilometres in a day.

Under the gathering gloom of the afternoon, winds whip up funnels of loose prairie, making life difficult for everything but the ubiquitous horse-flies. The sheep begin to stir anxiously. Gathered around a waterhole, the half-acre of crowded dusty wool begins to move into action. Creating a weaving mass of undulating carpet that lifts a low dirt cloud, they let out a universal baaaaah.

That brings the whistle, usually hanging on a string around his neck, up to O'Brien's mouth. A growl of thunder rolls in from the horizon as Gem and Snuffy leap into action. Responding to O'Brien's varying whistle tones, the dogs take up positions close to the flock, steering would-be strays back to the main group.

"You're only as good as your best dog in this business," he says.

Good dogs don't come cheap. Maybe $1,000 to $4,000 will get you a good dog, but there are no guarantees. You buy the breeding, explains O'Brien. But the breeding sometimes isn't passed on through the whole litter; he should know, being a longtime collie breeder.

Gathering up that many sheep and directing them into their pen at night, or rounding them up for periodic injections against blackleg or scepticaemia, takes the efforts of at least two good dogs. From herding sheep to chasing off the appetites of wandering coyotes, border collies are a great breed for the job.

"Coyotes can mean problems, but this year we've had little trouble. One of my dogs got a licking from a coyote last week, but they've kept away from us since then."

O'Brien has to face other problems that are closer to home. This cowboy has a fair share of bad weather out here alone with the elements. Trees and other shelter potential are few and far between, and if O'Brien is far from the small camper unit he uses to sleep in at nights, he has to make do with a small clump of buck-brush, or take his chances under his broad-brimmed hat.

"My wife got me one of those Australian slickers this year, didn't want me coming back every weekend soaking wet," he laughs.

His flock belongs to about 20 sheep producers, operating under a joint project by the Saskatchewan Sheep Development Board and the PFRA. For the past three years, the producers have paid for their sheep to use the Elbow-Willner pasture, about an hour and a half's drive south of Saskatoon. It's a program that benefits more than just the sheep producers.

The project was initiated as a response to leafy spurge, a noxious weed that seems to be loathed by the whole world, particularly pasture operators (where the plant can crowd out other plant growth favoured by cattle). Sheep, alone among the animal or human world, gobble up this yellow weed, thrilling both cattle and sheep producers.

"They'll hunt the stuff down and pass over any of the feed that cattle go for. It's like they're addicted to the stuff," O'Brien explains.

This means grazing grass, preferred by cattle, gets the opportunity to flourish when it has less competition from the leafy spurge. Studies indicate that when sheep graze in pastures that have infestations of the weed it could actually increase the amount of other feed available to cattle feeding in the same pasture.

For O'Brien, the wide-open spaces provide their own attraction. A local farmer and rancher for many years, sheep herding came along later in his life.

"I got interested in sheep through my love of dogs and in seeing them trained properly. I've always had a dog around and I started as a youngster, helping an American who travelled up here to train his bird dogs. I eventually graduated to working with sheep dogs."

So the cowboy turned shepherd and changed from watching over Herefords to guarding the likes of North Country Cheviots and Suffolks. In the fall he still helps out with the annual cattle roundup in the pasture, but he has gained a real respect for the sheep that he caretakes.

"Any job that gets me out in the fresh air is a big plus in my books. Cattle or sheep, it's my job to make sure they all stay healthy."

"Out of this bunch," he says, leisurely gazing out at the ranks of his rambling nomadic flock being persuaded along by Gem and Snuffy, "I've only lost two head in two months. That's a pretty low percentage and I plan on keeping it that way."

For most of trapper Noah Ballentyne's 67 years,
he has made his living in Saskatchewan's north.

Carving a Life
from the North Woods

It was -30° and the trapper's dark, swaddled shape was almost swallowed by the pristine snow as he broke trail through the tall tangle of white spruce trees that hid his small cabin. The log he carried under his arm must have weighed at least a quarter of his own body weight, but despite being bundled up in thick parka and heavy mitts, Noah Ballentyne made the task look easy enough.

Trapping is a tough and solitary occupation, a career not designed for the upwardly mobile or devotees of a soft, two-bathroom, centrally heated lifestyle, but Ballentyne appears well satisfied with his lot. While groups of Canadian aboriginal and Métis organizations fight it out with European Commission politicians who are planning to restrict the importation of North American pelts, he continues happily doing what he's done most of his life: trap. Tucked away in his northern Saskatchewan forest, thousands of kilometres away from the lofty halls of political power, Ballentyne is not thinking about the European drama; his mind is focused on a different kind of heat.

The log he's carrying, after he's cut it into stove-size pieces, will last until morning, sufficient to keep his tiny 13-square-metre cabin toasty warm, at least until dawn. But even before the last flickers of flame have died away, you can bet ice will have formed on the water pail in the drafty confines of his home. Then the ongoing search for more fuel for his ancient woodstove begins again; it's a daily chore the experienced woodsman takes in stride.

The forest and Ballentyne have been familiar with each other's company for a long time. For most of Noah's 67 years, the tough Cree has made his living from the dense woodlands of Saskatchewan's north country. For almost 20 years he worked the forests, chopping wood and hauling logs for pulp and lumber mills. For the past 12 years, he has run a trap line near Montreal Lake, seeking out lynx, wolves, coyotes, beaver, muskrat, and other fur-bearing animals that roam the forest.

He pays $10 for his annual trapping licence and $15 for the lease on his cabin. As for groceries, the slab of deer meat on a shelf in his kitchen is a further reflection of the trapper's low cash inputs for supplies. His needs are simple, which is just as well considering his limited income opportunities.

His is not a lucrative career path. With fur prices down, Ballentyne is lucky to collect $15 for a beaver pelt and maybe $20 for a fisher when he makes his infrequent trips into La Ronge to sell his season's work.

"But it keeps me out of trouble," he said. "The work is not as easy as it used to be, but I enjoy it. It's something I have always done, since I was a young boy."

With no motorized vehicle, truck, or snowmobile, he relies on his legs and a good pair of snowshoes in the winter. In the spring and fall, he has an old push-bike that transports him around his trapping territory.

His cabin is the height of simple function. A wash basin, small table, a single chair, covered sofa, and bed hug the room. The centrepiece of the one-room cabin has to be his old stove. His oil lamps are used sparingly to conserve fuel, as is the battery-fed radio that sits on his crowded table. With a long wire improvising as an antenna, the radio brings news and weather crackling from the outside. Other than a few books, it's his only form of entertainment.

The scene was not always a picture of this one-sided socialization. He used to keep a dog for company at his isolated spot, but over the previous couple of years wolf packs have taken two of his dogs.

While pragmatic enough to know the bounty of nature is without conscience, the fact Creation can bite both ways was enough for him to decide there'd be no more pet dogs in camp.

"The wolves will send a lone female in to get the attention of my dog. When my dog takes on after the wolf, the female leads him to the rest of the pack, and it's goodbye dog."

So Noah sticks with his solitude. He'll spend upwards of a week at a time at his cabin before coming out to spend a few days on his reserve at Little Red near Prince Albert. He says he enjoys the occasional companionship on the reserve, but he's always anxious to get back to his trap line and the primitive surroundings of his lonely log cabin.

The life is not for everyone, he agrees, but then again he couldn't stand living in the city. Having to tackle the fuss and fumes of that life is not for him. Everyone treads his own trail in life, he says, and the paths he walks are clear and uncluttered.

Larry Risling rounds them up on his Cadillac ranch.

Fleet Owner "Caddies"
—— Train Crews in Style ——

It's maybe not quite the Graceland garage, but Larry Risling's yard in Wilkie does hold more than a few echoes of Elvis's car fetish. Risling is the proud owner of seven immaculate white Cadillacs. While the numbers might not match the fleet size of the late pop star, it's an awesome sight for "Caddie" lovers when he lines them up in the courtyard of his home.

While Elvis's favourite car might also be Risling's top auto choice, the sleek lines of the automobiles aren't just pretty faces to the grain farmer. These Cadillacs are the workhorses for the dead-head transportation service he and his son, Randy, operate in this west-central region for the CP Rail system.

Wilkie is an important link in the CP freight network. Its rail lines are busy with a vibrant cross-country traffic that carries everything from Oldsmobiles and Hondas to the less glamourous, but equally profitable, loads of potash and grain.

Over the years the CP line has become a crucial part of the town's financial health. Its strategic position has enabled Wilkie to become a terminus for CP crews operating trains out of Hardisty, about 200 kilometres to the west across the Alberta border, and Saskatoon, about 180 kilometres to the east.

Driving replacement train crews to work and bringing off-duty crews home is what his deadhead service is all about. Easier on the crews and their families, and more economical and efficient than the bunkhouses of the past, the system minimizes the amount of time CP staff spend away from their homes. For the past six years Risling and the hired drivers of his Cadillac deadhead service have safely shuttled the trains' engineers, conductors, and brakemen among the three communities.

When he began his business in 1989 he'd opted for passenger vans to transport the crews. They proved expensive to operate so he looked at alternative vehicle types. He did not have to look far. It was an easy choice for Risling when it came to selecting which vehicle would replace the vans.

"I've always had a soft spot for a Cadillac. They are tough and they are well made and, I've got to confess, it's an easy car to fall in love with," he says.

Usually carrying between two and four passengers, the Cadillacs, driven by Risling and the six part-time drivers he employs, have proven a very reliable and surprisingly economic mode of transport over the past five years. The vehicle makes the round trip to Hardisty in about four hours, somewhat less for the journey between Wilkie and Saskatoon. The total annual travel of the fleet amounts to over 160,000 kilometres.

Purchased used, but with low mileage and well maintained, Risling's Cadillac fleet includes two-door and four-door models as well as a regal-looking 1986 limousine. Dependable, solid, and comfortable, the vehicle's elegance, however, is not a great consideration for Risling as far as his business enterprise is concerned.

"It's the folks that we move from point A to point B that matter in this business, and I don't think they give a darn about what the vehicles they travel to work in look like. As long as they are safe and comfortable, that's all that matters. Besides, most of the time they are fast asleep within minutes of climbing into the car."

Mike and Elaine Mahoney rely on the wild rice harvest to provide some Christmas cash.

The Wild Rice Harvest Is a World Apart

The morning had started well: crisp, bright with the promise of a warm day hidden somewhere in the chilly dawn. Mike and Elaine Mahoney spread the bright blue tarp across the soggy shoreline and stood waiting, reflectively smoking cigarettes as they watched for the arrival of the harvester that was buzzing through a thick stand of wild rice a kilometre down the lake. Breaking the silence of the wilderness, the distant noise of the airboat harvester ebbed and flowed, echoing its strains across the smooth waters.

The Mahoneys have been working on the wild rice harvest for the past five weeks. Today they are on bagging detail. They will spend the morning filling sacks with the raw wild rice harvested by the aluminum airboat that skims atop the water, knocking the mature rice kernels into its broad pickup.

The small skiff they piloted into this lake through a narrow connecting creek will carry the 30-kilogram sacks of rice back to their home base about five kilometres away. After a few days of harvesting, when there are enough bags, a radio call into La Ronge will bring in a Twin Otter to fly out the product and the rice will be processed for market.

The dull roar of the harvester had changed to a piercing scream as the propeller-powered machine moved towards the couple, its wild rice load brimming up the sides of the pickup. Nudging up to Mike and Elaine on shore, it was quickly emptied of its load by the couple, who scooped the rice out onto the tarp. In five minutes, the harvester had pulled away and they began the laborious task of filling the bags.

They chattered about this and that while they worked together, once in a while laughing quietly at some private joke, but all the time their hands were busy moving rice from tarp to sack. The fall colours of the forest reflected brightly in the still waters of the lake, and a season that holds a double-edged sword—the promise of death and rebirth—provided a serene backdrop to the busy harvesting scene.

Mike and Elaine work for Riese's Wild Rice, a La Ronge-based company that is the largest independent producer in the province. Mike says it's a good job, interesting work, but more important, one that puts money on the table.

To survive in Canada's northland takes some ingenuity. Not that the couple need lessons in bush survival. Both were born in northern Saskatchewan and the forests hold few secrets for them. It's economic survival that's increasingly the bottom line for northern families like the Mahoneys.

Their trap line usually provides a reasonably healthy income, but it was a bad year. The traps yielded sufficient fur, but falling demand and low prices brought a shortfall in their expected income. Mike has made good money over the years linecutting for exploration companies checking out the mineral wealth of the province. But there's little exploration these days—another dried-up well, as far as employment is concerned.

That's why the six- or seven-week northern wild rice harvest is so important to the couple. Making good cash this time of year means a good Christmas for them and their four children. Waiting for the harvester to return, Elaine shows off pictures of her family standing around their beautiful hand-built log home on Upper Foster Lake.

Living in so isolated a spot (their home is about 220 kilometres north of La Ronge) might have some drawbacks, but for peace and quiet and spectacular scenery, its the only place to be for this couple.

The youngest child is five and away at boarding school farther south, the last one to leave the nest, says Elaine nostalgically. So for the Mahoneys, the fall harvest season is also bittersweet. By Christmas, however, they will be together again and no doubt will make the most of it.

In the distance the muffled racket of the harvester gathers vocal force as the machine makes its way slowly back to the two baggers. There's just time for another shared cigarette before the driver comes in with another load.

Life is simple up here. Bosnia, constitutional wrangles, money markets, and social upheaval seem far away from this peaceful world. Even the modern noise from the approaching harvester seems to have all the power of a falling pin in a cathedral.

Domenico Fiorante, from Regina, knows what it's like to lug around crates of grapes.

Wine-makers
─── Preserve Their Heritage ───

Outside the Canadian-Italian Club in Regina, the rain fell and a cold wind held stern notice of winter. No matter, the grapes from sunny California had just arrived.

It was time to make wine, and the half-tons, vans, and cars of the club's members lined up to take on board the fixings for this year's batch of vino. Frail wooden packing cases holding grenache, alicante, muscat, and a couple of other varieties of plump, sweet grapes were stacked high under the heavy drizzle, waiting claim by their new owners.

While you can take an Italian out of Italy, you can't take Italy out of a Canadian Italian. Even here, deep in the Prairies where wheat is king, the age-old custom of wine-making lingers on in the blood of these people from southern Europe. As the province's grain harvest, beset by foul weather, stutters under way, out in northern California there were no such problems. Fall traditionally is time for the harvesting of the grape and the consequent squeezing of the precious fruit to make the elixir we call wine.

The fact that you live in a place where the nearest vineyard is 1,200 kilometres away doesn't change the fact that it's time to make wine. Two truckloads of grapes—2,000 cases—as well as another load of fresh grape juice had made their way from the golden state to the club's parking lot. For the past 10 years, the club has organized this form of grape relief for the amateur wine-makers among its membership.

And there are lots of them. Dominic Dipaola figures about 130 wine-makers ordered grapes or juice this year. Dipaola, who works at the club, will make about 30 gallons of wine himself.

"I'm making it from juice this year, not the grapes. It's too much trouble, all that messing around is no good. With juice most of the work's done for you," he says, filling out a receipt for a customer.

It costs $33 for a 25-litre pail, not bad considering that works out to about $1.25 a bottle for the finished item. The grapes (O sole Mio brand—what else?) weigh in at a little more than 13 kilograms a case and cost $16.50. It takes two cases of grapes to produce about 25 litres of juice.

The trend might be towards the easier juice method, but there are many traditionalists who stick to using grapes.

"I like to squeeze them with my feet, that way I get my feet washed for nothing," jokes Silvano Carani as he crowds 22 cases of golden crassela, muscat, and other grape choices in the back of his half-ton.

Carani speaks in jest. His wine-making actually is well organized. Modern equipment and a family team that includes Diva, his wife, and a son-in-law who married into the wine-making family will produce about 225 litres of wine this year. It's a long way (in more ways than just distance) from the countryside around Florence to the suburban streets of Saskatchewan's Queen City, but the presence of wine at mealtimes is a way of life for the Carani family.

Since he left the farm in the Italian countryside and came to Canada in 1959, Silvano has continued making his wine the way he saw his parents produce it in the old country.

"All of it is natural," he says, his smooth-flowing Italian accent still very noticeable. "No chemicals or preservatives, it's just the real thing."

More vehicles arrive and this corner of Regina becomes a little Italy. The wine-makers' native language, in several dialects, flows as fast and as clear as good Chianti at an Italian wedding.

Despite the incessant rain and thick cloud that hangs over the Canadian-Italian Club, somehow there's a shock of southern sunshine falling on this crowd of expectant amateur vintners. The weather might not be so good for the poor Saskatchewan farmer, but it could be a vintage year for a few dozen basement wine-makers.

Stan Dudek carved the Whitetail resort out of the rolling hillside northeast of the Battlefords.

On the Trail
of a Dream

A t this time of year the sun is swallowed all too quickly by the soft, undulating contours of the Thickwood Hills. Still, the short days hold their own rewards in the dazzling light show of deep blues, golds, pinks, and purples as day moves into night.

Stan Dudek has been a watcher of sunsets over this land for as long as he can remember; it's a sight he never tires of. Maybe that's why he decided to hang his hat on the nearest stand around, and set up shop right on the land where he was born and raised. "Shop" is actually the Whitetail ski resort—40 kilometres of cross-country ski trails, groomed and trimmed to perfection, which course their way through 3,500 acres of rolling hills northeast of the Battlefords.

Shortly after high school Stan had moved to Alberta to follow his first love, the rugged outdoors. Managing a hostel, mountain guiding, survival training: Stan was challenged by the path he had chosen far from the prairie of his childhood. The process would deepen not only his love for Canada's wilderness areas, but also play a major part in shaping his character.

He was still in his early 20s by the time he left his job as a hostel custodian in the Alberta Rockies, returning to Saskatchewan to help his parents run the family farm, about 30 kilometres north of Denholm. After his experiences in the Rockies, his eventual return to farm chores proved less than exciting. Driving a tractor, herding cattle, and all the other day-to-day chores meant time hung heavy on the young farmer who had tasted a different kind of freedom in the mountains.

At that time, with the Saskatchewan farm economy in a deepening malaise, Stan's folks decided that a large area of their rolling pasture land would become more productive if the heavy bush on the property was removed.

"I wasn't going to do that. I'd hiked those hills as a kid and fished in the creeks. There had to be something that we could do to make that property viable," Stan told me last week, after I'd travelled up to share a local sunset with him.

So he took out a loan, bought the land, and began working on a scheme that would make the pasture more productive; agriculture would take on much less significance in the final picture.

"I love to ski and had the idea that the sport had some potential for growth. I suppose it was natural that I looked at developing the place into a cross-country ski resort."

In 1988 he angled a Cat through the bush to make a path that would become his first ski trail. Later he would develop more trails along the tree-covered slopes, grooming them carefully and tailoring them to the needs of novice to advanced skiers.

"My father would wonder why I wanted to develop this spot when it was such poor land, only good for cattle. I saw things very differently, I suppose. As far as farming was concerned, I didn't have my heart in it, but I did have a dream of making a resort out of all this land."

So, despite some parental skepticism, Stan went ahead with his dream, and Whitetail moved off the mental drawing board and became a three-dimensional reality. Every year came new improvements, paid for by Stan's farm income. A chalet, cabins for overnight accommodation, public showers, and a biathlon range began to take shape as Stan's energies tuned into the needs of an expanding clientele. These days those sunsets are seen by more and more people who travel from as far away as Alberta to experience the thrill of Stan's cross-country ski trails.

Still only 30, the enthusiasm flows just as strong in Stan's blood, although his productivity is edged with a powerful respect for the land around him. Maintaining his property as a ski resort, and carefully blending his trails into the surrounding landscape, ensures the land stays pretty well in its natural state, and that fits into the entrepreneur's plans just fine.

"I was setting track the other day, and right in front of me a snowy owl swooped down and picked up a rabbit that was crossing the ski track and took off, just like that," he explained.

Money is not a big factor in the young bachelor's plans. If it had been, he says, developing a ski resort would not have been a viable option.

"My parents are puzzled how I get by financially, but I manage just fine. I'm convinced that planning around money is destructive in the long run. I'd sooner come to terms with life on a day-to-day basis."

It's at the close of those days, when the skiers are coming to the end of their runs, and the sun begins to hit the crease of the surrounding hills that Stan can take a little time away from his chores. That's when he can take a breather from his duties at the concession stand, the ski rental facility, or the thousand and one fix-it problems that absorb a lot of his time, and look up to view a scene that money can't buy.

Cyril Golding surveys oat field near Borden.

Ninety Years of
——— Crop-season Memories ———

W hen you are over 90, chances are you've seen some cold, cold summers, but 1992's climatic debacles have them all stumped. That's what Cyril Golding, a retired Borden farmer reckons. Golding will be 91 in November. He's seen pretty well everything the gods can hurl at a nicely ripening choice field of Saskatchewan grain.

"In '37 I had 500 acres of land planted. It was so dry that year all the crop I took off from my work I could have put in my hat," remembers Golding. Not that it mattered much. Like today's suffering farm scene, prices were not the best. Back then you would get about 20 cents a bushel for best-quality Number 1 Northern.

"But I guess we survived somehow," says Golding.

In 1935 he married, right in the middle of the Great Depression. Not the best of timing as far as finances were concerned, what with businesses and farms biting the dust all across the province.

"But love is love," he explains.

It was a very good marriage by all accounts. When Cyril's wife died in 1985, it left a huge gap in his life. From time to time, he still struggles with that reality. However, at the altar 57 years ago, Cyril's "I do" was almost an "I almost do." The economy was so bad, the cash they had squeezed together barely covered the cost of the preacher and the wedding photograph.

Not that money had ever been spilling out of the young Golding's pockets. In 1903, he had arrived in Saskatchewan as a two-year-old with his parents. They had left England for a life that held the vague hope of prosperity.

"Hope is a funny word. It's always something out there, never here, nothing you can take to the bank," Golding smiles at his own philosophy. On their new homestead in the Blaine Lake area, they found raw prairie, bush, and a lot of loneliness.

"We were probably the only white family west of the North Saskatchewan River at that time."

Eventually, they moved closer to Borden and got into the real business of farming, and all the ups and downs of rural life that are played out against the backdrop of weather and grain prices. So it is with some tempered experience that Golding listens to this year's crop reports. In some prairie regions this season, grain kernels, littered with the angst of frost and rain, are moulding, sprouting, shrinking, and shrivelling towards near-disaster.

Hearing that probably 40 percent of this year's grain crop has been affected by cold and damp brings back more memories for Golding. The year after his marriage was also the growing season his in-laws sported a wheat crop that was so good it could have been framed and put in a picture. That was, however, before the midnight hailstorm late in July that left the field as clean as a whistle.

"You couldn't have found a standing stalk anywhere in that field, and I helped plant that crop."

Through the years, it was like that. Good crops, bad crops, mediocre crops, no crop at all: farming was so unpredictable that Golding moved on to doing custom ploughing, seeding, and combining.

"That way the risk wasn't all mine," he says.

Golding fought the hard times by gradually getting out of farming and into several businesses that helped put bread on the table. House moving, hauling fuel, installing sewer and water lines, they were all ways of making a go at living on the Prairies. That's a pattern he hopes other farmers don't follow. We need farmers more than ever, he explains. It's a way of life that is the backbone of society, he says. Even at 90, Golding is never too far from a grain field. An active member of the local threshing club, he and other volunteers are planning their sixth annual threshing festival at Borden.

"And it's going ahead even if it stays as cold as it's been. This is one crop we're going to get off," he says.

Lorne Swenson gets an appreciative nudge from his lead dog, Lingo.

Sledding Marries Interests
—— in Dogs and the Outdoors ——

B
ack in the compound on his acreage the two pensioners were howling like hounds from hell as Lorne Swenson hooked his other dogs to his racing sled. The 12-year-old sled dogs are retired from the race circuit, but Swenson's oldest canines still have competitive blood in their veins, judging by the racket they make. While the two dogs are no longer part of Swenson's race team, they still have a place in the 44-year-old musher's heart.

"I could never get rid of any of them; they are just too close to me," he says.

While he talks, Swenson hitches up his dog team to a harness stretched out in front of a sleek-looking sled anchored to his half-ton. Taking each dog in turn out of cages on the back of his truck he chats to his charges. Each dog has a name and a temperament.

"Come on, Montana, let's have you out. This one's called Shy, he's quiet but a good puller. How are you doing, Lingo?" He handles the dogs gently and gets a few damp, cold noses shoved into his face in appreciation.

Swenson is getting ready for one of the big dog races to be held at Prince Albert's Winter Festival. Featured this year is a new dog race, and it's heavily underlined in Lorne Swenson's calendar. "The P.A. 180" Sled Dog Derby—a 290-kilometre race to and from Nipawin will be run on 20 February from Prince Albert. After an overnight rest in Nipawin the mushers will race back to Prince Albert.

A forestry technician by profession, Swenson took up his sled dog racing hobby about 10 years ago. A love for the outdoors and for dogs pulled him into the sport by accident.

"I used to have a husky who would pull my wife and me around while we were on cross-country skis. I guess that's where I first became interested," he says. His hobby does not come cheap. A minimum price for a dog hits around $500, while a good lead dog can set you back more than $2,000. As well, racing dogs can eat through as much as $175 of feed a month.

What does Wendy, Swenson's wife, think of his dog sled racing?

"She's not that fond of it, but she's the major sponsor of my expensive hobby, which she allows me to continue."

About three years ago he switched from the shorter races to the gruelling long-distance ones as far away as Alberta and Manitoba. When you're in the middle of a 350-mile race you really appreciate having a good dog team. Strength, intelligence, and spirit are the characteristics to check out in sled dogs, Swenson says.

When you are running anywhere from 6 to 10 dogs, it's crucial the dogs work well together, he explains. Out on the track, in the middle of nowhere, the musher needs all his concentration to control his team. You really live in the now, Swenson says.

"It's the part I enjoy. There's just the trail, the dogs, the sled, and me. You really need to stay focused in this game."

Tom Thomas "spoons up" a variety of intricate designs.

The Welsh Literally "Spoon" on Moonlit Nights

For young romantics in Wales, spooning on moonlit nights has been taken literally for the past 400 years. While most of us might be satisfied sending love notes, cards, or flowers to our intended, Welshmen would busy themselves with chisel and knife carving wooden spoons—love spoons—as a token of their feelings.

Colonsay resident Tom Thomas explains that a young man in Wales would announce his interest in a young female by painstakingly hand-shaping an ornate wooden spoon and delivering the utensil in person. Presumably, the more intricate the carving and the more complicated the design, the more love was being expressed. Thomas says if the young woman accepted the spoon it meant the feeling of interest was mutual.

"The carving of Welsh love spoons is a true ethnic craft," Thomas says in his deep Welsh accent.

It's a craft that's close to the 69-year-old's heart. For the past 10 years Thomas has developed love spoon carving from a hobby into a small business. From the basement of his house in this small community, about 70 kilometres east of Saskatoon, Thomas has produced hundreds of spoons of all shapes and sizes. He sells them at local craft fairs and sales.

"Now that I'm retired I have a lot of time on my hands, particularly in winter. It's more something to do, really," the former construction worker says.

Since he was a youngster he had thought he would one day get to carve love spoons. While he worked professionally as a stone mason, farm worker, and carpenter in his native Wales he admired the craftsmanship in love spoon carving. He also was attracted to the theme of the endeavour. Love is universal, he says.

"I never knew I would have to first leave Wales in order to be able to find time to work at making these spoons, though."

It was 10 years ago that Thomas and his wife, Nona, decided to emigrate to Canada. They were following the path of their only son, who had been hired by the local potash mine near Colonsay. Retirement in a new country brought with it the necessary time needed to develop his hobbies: gardening in summer and carving love spoons in winter.

The best wood for carving spoons has a close, even grain, such as sycamore, lime-wood, birch, poplar, and walnut. Thomas says wood with a coarser grain, such as oak, ash, or cedar, can also be used but will not allow for detailed carving.

Using tiny chisels, a scroll saw, and a scooping knife, Thomas shapes his spoons to the required size and shape. Intricate designs and symbols are the most difficult to do, he explains. It can take six to eight hours to complete some of the more complex designs.

Carving in the spoon carries true messages the would-be suitor wants to express. Hearts are for love, links for the number of children desired, a keyhole for the door of the heart, and flowers mean gentleness. Thomas says spheres in a wooden cage mean trapped love, a ship means a happy life, and an anchor represents home.

Dickson Hardie's collection includes fossils of fish, prehistoric birds,
multi-million-year-old turtles, and other ancient dwellers of an ancient ocean.

Bone Hunting
along the Carrot River

His neighbours, living under the shadow of the same prairie elevators, had thought Dickson Hardie a pretty conservative farmer, until he mentioned the sharks' teeth he'd found on his land.

"There were some smiles and chuckles, not to mention more than a few belly laughs," he says, reflecting on the discovery of the first fossils on his farm, about 300 kilometres northeast of Saskatoon.

That was about 20 years ago. Today there's no laughing at the curious finds Hardie makes along the narrow banks of the Carrot River, which bends and curves its way along the border of his farm.

Fossils of fish, prehistoric birds, multi-million-year-old turtles, and other ancient dwellers of a more-ancient ocean that once covered this area, have been discovered by Hardie.

It was back in the mid-'70s when Hardie became seriously interested in the fossil potential of land that had previously held only agricultural value for him. He's not exactly sure why his fascination with the new pursuit of "bone hunting" took him away from his regular farming operation. His interest in paleontology came out of nowhere, according to the 81-year-old bachelor.

"One day I just began poking around down by the river, and moving a bit of dirt here and there," Hardie says.

Possibly he had reached the age where he was getting ready to retire from farming. More likely the call of a river, where he had spent so many happy times, became too strong to ignore. Anyway, all he concedes is that one day he stepped out of his tractor and into the world of paleontology.

It's a world that begins and ends for him on the banks of the Carrot River. Hardie says he heard they called it the Carrot because of the wild carrots that grew in the vicinity. Not a noble name, not like its neighbouring river, which early pioneers had christened the Jordan.

"Because it was supposed to be the promised land on the other side," he laughs.

But it was the Carrot River that held the real promise for Hardie. Maybe that's why he was silent as he stood on its bank, staring down at the slim band of slow-moving water edging comfortably along his farmland.

He swam this river, boated, and fished from its shores. It was a place for family picnics and evening walks, and amid the crowded memories of youth he had remembered finding evidence of an earlier time. Fossils from an age when the river had been part of an ocean; a place where long-extinct birds, reptiles, and fish had swooped, slithered, and lived out their lives. He'd seen them and ignored them.

"It's not much to look at now. It used to be cleaner and deeper; now it's pretty well a dead river. You wouldn't want to eat the fish out of here," he says.

Before he'd made the familiar 300-metre trip from his front door to the riverbank that day he'd already shown me his extensive collection of fossils. The traces of ancient plants and animals preserved in rocks are spread neatly on a double-level display table in his kitchen, like an extensive dessert tray. He's still hunting fossils to add to his collection, despite the fact he's almost blind—"busted blood vessel behind my eyes or something," he tells me.

"My eyes started failing about five years ago and gradually got worse. The doctors can't do anything about it, but I'm not complaining. I can still stumble around."

He smiles towards the river. His jacket still shows the dried mud from a fall he had the day before on yet another exploration.

"Slid in the muck and my foot caught a root, and down I went. Could have been worse."

Despite his poor eyesight, he continues to make regular tours of his river edge. Feeling for what he can no longer see, mysteriously he still manages to come up with new finds.

"With my eyes the way they are it's harder to find stuff, but I still manage. That's just as well. You have to keep busy at a hobby after you retire or you'd go stale."

His hobby had started slowly, but after about five years of "poking around" Hardie was impressed enough by the significance of his finds that he consulted the science world. While unconcerned by the skeptics in the neighbourhood, he felt some confirmation on the potential of his finds was in order. In 1979, he sent a couple of boxes of fossil samples to the University of Saskatchewan.

"I couldn't get much of a response from them, figured they weren't interested. No matter—I still knew what I'd found could mean this place might be significant," he explains.

Undaunted by this setback, Hardie carried out his own personal research and field work. Using an old screwdriver, and once in a while a shovel, he continued to scrape and dig into the mud and dirt at the edge of the river, slowly adding to his collection. However, in the end he was to get his scientific recognition. In 1990, a team from the Royal Saskatchewan Museum arrived in the area on a surveying mission, Hardie recalls. When they examined his collection of fossils they were intrigued.

"It feels good when the experts tell you what you have found is like gold," Hardie says, flushing a little at the memory.

"I'm only a farmer; I don't have no degree or anything. I suppose you could say I have a knack for finding this stuff," he says, passing over a copy of the latest edition of *Equinox* magazine someone has sent him.

There's an article about the significance of one of the more recent finds made by the same paleontologists who had checked out Hardie's treasure trove. "Big Bert" died about 92 million years ago, but the fossil remains of the marine crocodile—called teleorhinus—is one of the best-preserved specimens of its kind. It was found on Hardie's land in the fall of 1991, along the edge of the Carrot River, less than three kilometres from his two-storey farmhouse. "Big Bert" has since been the object of extensive research. Compared to the small suckers and pike that can still be found in his river, Hardie says Bert was definitely a whopper. Museum scientists in Regina estimate its length to have been around seven metres.

"It's hard to think something like that could have been flourishing around these parts," he says, glancing at the surrounding landscape—a contrasting mix of heavy bush and cleared fields that sweep towards the river's edge.

There have been other important finds since, each confirming that the Carrot River area is a proven rich and valuable source of fossil presence. Hardie feels vindicated. His neighbours no longer smile at the thought that sharks, crocodiles, and exotic fish might have once patrolled their canola fields.

His enthusiasm for his hobby is still high. While he might have slowed down some in his exploring, Hardie still gets out for a few hours most days along his river; searching for more elusive quarry for his collection. That causes some concern among family members who tell him to let them know when he goes on his searches.

"They're worried I might not come back," he smiles. "That wouldn't be too bad, though. Maybe someday, 50 million or so years from now, someone would find my bones embedded in a bunch of rocks. That would leave 'em guessing."

Father Robert Gannon leads his solitary existence near Muenster.

A Hermit's Life
Is a Journey Inward

The weather and the landscape looked bleak. Snow was falling and the hard skeletons of trees seemed to skulk across the landscape as I drove towards the hermit's house. It was almost two years since I'd last visited my friend Father Robert Gannon. For the past 21 years, the Camaldolese monk has spent his life as a hermit in the countryside near Muenster, about 120 kilometres east of

Saskatoon. It was time to find out how his life was going.

Gannon was waiting for me as I pulled into the entrance of the yard. His face held a warm smile as he opened the door of the porch to welcome me in. Patched blue jeans, winter boots repaired with packing tape, and an open necked shirt—he's a dresser a-la-country-casual when he receives visitors.

His house would be in the category below what even the most optimistic real estate agent might call "functionally cosy." Settled into a bush-edged niche of open prairie in sight of St. Peter's Abbey, the tiny house is in definite need of a paint job. But at 61, Father Robert Gannon takes little heed of cosmetics. The qualities of latex and oil-based paints are not part of his thought patterns. His requirements are minimal, as can be shown by the contents of his 300-square-foot home.

A neat stack of freshly cut wood shares his tiny office/bedroom. A narrow bed, desk and chair, wood-stove, and his tall, sparse frame share the rest of the space. In his mini-kitchen, a fridge, freezer, and one-man table are all the comforts of home. A single-burner hot-plate sees to his culinary needs.

His life of self-imposed isolation and solitude allows him to focus: to carry out his purpose of prayer and his object of seeking a closer connection with his God. All the rest would be clutter. Distanced from those ego events that pull on the energies for most of the rest of us—money, possessions, and power—his is a journey inward.

He realizes there are people who might argue that he should move from prayer to action, that he should, like many other priests and religious, work within the community. These critics would not understand his belief in the power of prayer.

"My faith also brings with it the knowledge that my prayers do good, that they are being heard. So I don't see my time as being wasted."

He was born in Texas, the son of a middle-class lawyer. He would have followed the same lifestyle, but for the spiritual search that eventually brought him to a life with a religious order in California. Gannon came to Muenster because of a growing need to develop his prayer life beyond what was possible in the monastery he had helped build at Big Sur. Through an arrangement with the abbot at the Benedictine monastery of St. Peter's, he set up life as a hermit on the Saskatchewan prairies.

It would seem a hard life for most of us. While his accommodation is spartan, his regimen is no less challenging. His daily prayers begin at 3 A.M. sounded off by an alarm clock that sits at the side of his cot. Throughout the day he has regular extensive periods for mass and prayers, fitting his other activities into free time slots. He cuts his own firewood, plants his own garden, and goes for a lengthy daily walk.

"I never get lonely and I have never felt bored for many, many years," he told me.

We talked about many issues during the time I spent with Gannon. You can forget about cars, specific political issues, and fashions when you're with this man, although theological and philosophical matters emerge with ease. Divorce, abortion, poverty, war, the topics evoke great passion in him.

I enjoy my visits to this gentle man of God. In a world that increasingly seems to be upside-down and inside-out, it's good to find solid ground. My visits also serve to remind me of the energy of this hermit's prayer life.

Gannon gets discouraged sometimes. I suspect while he's mystically beyond most everyday happenings in the world he agonizes over big and small injustices, both on his doorstep and around the globe.

"But if we have enough faith, maybe there are no real tragedies," he muses. "Maybe in all acts and events there are lessons we have to learn. And that's the great mystery."

It's also good to know there is someone out there who prays to help move a universe in the right direction. It's a chance for me to get a glimpse of the big picture, even if it is seen through someone else's powerful faith.

Floss and Stan Graber with cowboy memorabilia.

Old Cowboy Stories
Relived

A rm in arm, the couple walks slowly down for an early dinner in the restaurant of the Senior Citizens' condominium complex. Stan and Floss Graber have been married 65 years, and the sight of the two lovebirds would restore even a cynic's belief in the benefits of the marital bond.

"We've had a good life together, and it's getting even better," says Stan, gently squeezing Floss's hand.

However, discovering his obvious domestic bliss was not the reason I had wanted to meet up with Stan in his Saskatoon condo. I'd been planning on visiting him for quite some time, to explore his experiences as a cowboy back in the early days of ranching in the province. At 91, Stan's days of herding prime Hereford beef cattle have long since passed, but I knew his memory was still sharp as prairie thistle.

Born on a ranch in North Dakota, he learned to ride at an age when shoelaces were still giving him problems. When his family moved to a Saskatchewan homestead, around 1906, horses continued to play a major role in the young boy's life.

As a youngster he'd managed to combine a keen business acumen—a talent that would pay off in later life—with his love of being in the saddle. Hooking up with a telegraph operator in Smiley, a small town northwest of Kindersley, he made a deal to deliver telegrams to the surrounding homesteaders—for a fee of course.

"I guess you could call it an amateur pony express, but it was a way for a poor farm boy to make a little cash," Stan says.

Old Bob was the name of the horse that carried Stan in those days. There have been many horses since then and Stan remembers them all, and their idiosyncracies.

"I rode horses that were good at night time, could find their way in a blackout, and others that were wonderful at sorting out cattle but would get lost as soon as the sun went down. I had this one horse who had a kink in the right side of his neck, and that's the direction he would always turn given half a chance," he chuckles. Horses and Stan were inseparable, that was until a day in his early 20s, when he exchanged his saddle for a pen and began his business career in a small bank in Elrose.

"Actually I have no regrets over my choice; I was pretty successful," he smiles. "But I sometimes wonder what would have happened if I would have stayed ranching."

But Stan, even in his tenth decade of life, has no trouble reconnecting with his horse wrangling days on the old Matador ranch in west-central Saskatchewan. The 140,000-acre spread of Saskatchewan prairie was assembled in 1903 by the largest multinational operation of its kind in the world, the Matador Land and Cattle Company. The Colorado-based corporation owned property all over the world, from Saskatchewan Landing to Brazil, and the teenaged cowpuncher was as pleased as punch to be riding the massive spread south of Elrose. Stan started with the Matador when he was 18, riding herd across the rough country of coulees, river flats, and buttes that made up much of the range.

"Our family ranch was pretty small, so this was heaven for someone like me. The fellows I rode with were a great bunch of guys, although you often didn't even know their last names or where they came from."

Stan says there was a great camaraderie among the cowpunchers. Sitting around the campfire or chuckwagon, chewing on sourdough biscuits, beans, and bacon, and listening to tales of cattle rides and rustling gangs that roamed the district, was soul food for a young mind.

Herding dogies and driving cattle between pasture lands were all part and parcel of Stan's job. On one memorable drive, he helped move more than 3,500 head of cattle 500 kilometres south to Montana, fording creeks, streams, and rivers in the process.

"We only lost one steer during the whole of that drive, remarkable really," he says.

It's those stories that are relived for Stan's readers in his regular column in the popular farm journal *Grain News*. Tumbleweed, being driven through deep coulees by a hard-driving northwest wind, flashing spurs, sleek sweating horses, and "the best bunch of cowpunchers this side of the Rockies" are all grist for the mill of Stan's word processor.

"They approached me about three years ago to write the column. It's been a wonderful excuse for me to recall the fun I had back then, and now I have the time to write about it."

Stan has long since retired from the business path he chose back in his 20s. That busy career, centred around a directorship with Bowman Brothers, a Saskatoon-based wholesale automotive supplier, was financially successful. But while he has fond memories of his business experiences, the days when he rode the unfenced prairie are remembered most vividly, he tells me.

"Maybe I'll get a book out of it, eventually," he says.

No doubt, recalling in Technicolored reality the events of youth is the rich comfort that old age gradually hands to the lucky ones among us. I'm grateful Stan's around to share the history with us. (Graber did go on to write *The Last Roundup*, also published by Fifth House.)

Florence Fusedale and her daughter Dorcas Oleskiw ensure that a family mincemeat tradition passes to another generation.

Mincemeat Bee
— Brings This Family Together —

You can always tell the good recipes when you look through someone's old cookbook; you find them on the pages spotted and speckled by a constant barrage of ingredient shrapnel.

I know, we have a recipe for dumplings that no member of the household has set eyes on over the past decade. That particular page in *The Joy of Cooking* has been fused to its neighbour with generous splashes of flour, eggs, and baking powder shotgunned around the kitchen through years of frenzied culinary enthusiasm.

Take the seasonal art of mincemeat making that some of the more ambitious cooks among us tackle every year. In tarts or pies, the rich ingredients that go into mincemeat are sure to bring wide smiles to guests visiting through the season. However, those same ingredients can also get downright messy in the kitchen, especially when quite a few members of the family are taking turns at stirring the pot.

When you have a look at the mincemeat recipe in Florence Fusedale's cookbook, you'll get an idea of what I mean. Now, there's a page where you can see a few generations of cooking activity spattered across the ingredient list. The page has taken on the identity more of a Rorschach test than directions for mincemeat manufacture.

But this particular list of ingredients is a time-proven formula for success, and Florence should know. Making mincemeat at Christmas has been a family custom in the Fusedale home for almost 50 years. The recipe is an even older family tradition, dating back to the early part of the century and written in her mother's cookbook that came out from England with Florence in 1928.

Put together in 1910, the well-used recipe book is a treasury of neatly hand-written cooking directions that includes such gems as jugged hare, stewed eels, Aberdeen sausage, coconut fingers, and of course the famous mincemeat recipe that's played such an important role in Florence's kitchen through the years.

Florence laughs when she recalls how, over those years, various members of her family have connected with the recipe in their own special way.

"When my husband was alive, he would also get into the act. It was his job to portion out the brandy that went into the recipe, and he'd inevitably add a few extra ounces to give it a lift," she explains.

Florence is 90, and blind, but astonishingly she still keeps her hand in the annual mincemeat preparation. With a little encouragement and some physical help from her family, she manages to turn out a hefty load of the heavy-duty dessert in time for Christmas.

Dorcas Oleskiw is Florence's daughter and care-giver, who continues to pass the skills of mincemeat preparation along to younger family members. This year, Dorcas's own daughter organized the ongoing passage of the famous recipe to yet another generation.

"She'd remembered the times she'd spent helping her grandmother making up batches of mincemeat before Christmas, and she wanted to get her own children involved, to pass along the experience," Dorcas said.

So this year, Florence had intergenerational help in the shape of two granddaughters and three great-grandchildren. This year's cooking bee proved beyond a doubt that when it comes to mincemeat preparation too many cooks do not spoil anything ... in fact, they enhance the process.

"The two young girls peeled and cored the apples, and the boy got a chance to show off his mechanical ability by operating the food processor. We all took turns mixing the ingredients," Florence said.

Exhausting as the multi-cook extravaganza was for the 90-year-old, the experience held its own rewards as new memories were planted in young minds.

"I think we gain a little immortality with such events," she said. "We live on through connections like this."

In the end it might only seem like a few jars of mincemeat, but sharing food and cooking chores, as well as the traditional coming together of family and friends, means something much more.

If you want to start your own cooking tradition, here's the original 1910 mincemeat recipe from Florence's cookbook.

Ingredients: 1 lb. beef suet, 1½ lb. stoned raisins (regular raisins will do), ¾ lb. cleaned currants, 1 lb. minced apples, 1 lb. demerara sugar, 2 oz. mixed peel, juice from 2 lemons, 1 tsp. pudding spice (substitute nutmeg and cloves), 1 oz. shelled and chopped sweet almonds, ¼ pint brandy or port.

Mix all the ingredients thoroughly and seal in containers. Allow to mellow for a few weeks in a cool place before using.

*Now retired, John Bowles uses his basement workshop to develop his own ideas,
such as this radio-controlled 1949 Pontiac.*

Welcome to John Bowles's Twilight Zone

He's in his basement workshop—his Twilight Zone—surrounded by stacks of Vogue tobacco cans, homemade electronic testing equipment, and the sound of his wife's voice echoing from the kitchen upstairs.

"Come upstairs, I've made a cup of tea," Vera Bowles pleaded. It was her third attempt in 20 minutes at persuading her husband to leave his work bench. After more than 55 years of marriage, she knows it's a fruitless task.

For a moment John Bowles was distracted, glancing up from the array of transistors, relay switches, and lines of wire that make up the workings of the scale-model 1949 radio-controlled car he's manufactured.

"She gets mad at me. Can't blame her, I suppose, but when I'm down here time seems to dissolve. I call it my Twilight Zone, and I could stay down here all day. Other than going up and washing a few dishes and saying an occasional hello to my wife, I could live my life here."

It's a strange heaven. Bathed in bright fluorescent light, the gauges, dials, and testing cables—the former eyes and ears of John Bowles's radio repair trade—take up most of the shelf space on his work bench. Taking up the rest of the cramped space are tobacco cans, salvage from a lifetime of smoking now given new life as storage containers for brass screws and relay contacts.

At 81, his fascination for making electrical ideas function is still running at full power. Born in England, he had his first experience of Canada and the prairies during the war, when he spent three years training to repair airplane radios. He met Vera, and they moved to England and his RAF career for the duration of the war, returning to Saskatchewan permanently in 1947.

For years he operated a Saskatoon home-based radio repair business, using the same basement workshop that has become his hideaway, during an active retirement an electronic escape route from the everyday anxieties of a modern world.

"I can come down here and suddenly my worries do not exist. If I have a bee in my bonnet here, it has to do with an idea I'm working on. I have to be interested in a project; it has to capture my imagination. Otherwise forget it."

His interests, while focusing on the world of electricity, have brought about a few quiet revolutions in the Bowles household. Take his kitchen table, for instance. When you look around the family kitchen you see the fridge, stove, cupboards, countertop, but no table. However, a press of a hidden button produces a slow whirring sound, and up from the floor a dinner table begins to emerge from the smooth, lino-covered floor.

"A 1952 invention, built to accommodate an expanding family in a small house," John explains modestly. "Powered by an airplane's bomb bay motor and worked by airplane cables, the table's gone up and down successfully for more than 40 years."

The table is an example of the typical precision and attention to detail John gives to any assignment to which he sets himself. He says all his ideas begin as visualizations in his mind long before they take shape on his bench. He taps the side of his head.

"I see it here, and I'll think about it for a long time. I never take shortcuts. My wife gets mad at me because she says I talk forever when I'm describing something. On and on I go, she says, but I'll tell you something about my style of explanation: by the time I've finished describing something you know exactly what it is, to a picture, what I'm talking about."

The radio-controlled '49 Pontiac also works like a charm. With a radio range of almost a kilometre, the vehicle can turn on a dime from directions passed along via his homemade control box. Even the heavy-duty batteries that power the trim car have been fashioned from scratch in his basement.

"When I build something I expect it to last, and when you put something together yourself you can control things like that."

His belief in permanence also extends to the family car. Bought new in 1949, his Austin still runs as smoothly as summertime honey, and is still his primary means of transportation. The vehicle is a source of pride and joy to him, a connection with the past and an obviously hot conversation piece. John begins to describe the first journey the little car made through the mountains, but is interrupted by his wife's voice.

"John, your tea is getting cold. Are you coming up?"

For just a second he pauses and looks towards the stairs. For a moment he appears de-activated.

"Okay, dear, just one more minute. Now where was I? I've lost my train of thought ... Oh yes, the car ... "

Mavis and Terry Ryan survey the damage caused by a disastrous fire.

Their Jobs Went
Up in Flames

Imagine watching your job go up in smoke. Terry Ryan and his wife Mavis did just that when the farm equipment and hardware store in Cut Knife burned to the ground.

"How do you describe the feelings that go through you when you see the place you've worked for 25 years collapsing around you?" says the 47-year-old Ryan, who had worked as a delivery driver at the doomed company, Finley's Auto and Farm Supply.

Mavis had worked in the busy hardware section of the successful store for more than 12 years. She says seeing the fire consume not only the building but her livelihood was mind-numbing. "Too unreal" to think about while it was happening.

But now, as the full trauma of the event has settled in, the Ryans, one of the three married couples who worked at what was the largest employer in this community of 600, realize they face an uncertain future. The 25 employees who lost their jobs can only look in disbelief at the gutted shell of the structure that scars the snow-covered street. But for owner Paul Finley it is all too real. It's the end of a business started by his father 66 years earlier.

Even now, despite the burned-out wreckage, business life goes on at the site. A giant car transporter unloads its cargo of cars under the Finley neon sign, about the only survivor of the blaze, while the owner handles the necessary paperwork.

"I'm 61, so I could see my retirement on the horizon, but what a hell of a way to leave business," he says, looking over the piles of blackened and crushed trucks, cars, and tractors that litter the skeletal remains of the family business.

It all happened so fast, he says. He heard the town's fire alarm from his office on the second floor of the structure and looked out of the window to see if he could spot any of the community's buildings on fire. Soon after that he heard the yells of fire and warnings to evacuate his company.

"I didn't even have time to so much as get a damn ballpoint out of the desk drawer."

While the unloading of the transporter gives the impression business is returning to normal, at least for the car dealership division of the enterprise, Finley says that's only an illusion. He's just winding up a few contracts and then the new cars will stop coming and he will close the doors for good on Finley's.

"That's if I had any doors left to close," he says ruefully.

He's too old to rebuild and start again. Even if he wanted to, the large automakers and farm implement suppliers are gradually changing marketing strategies and developing their dealerships in larger centres.

However, Paul Finley has been a good boss. Every worker will receive two months' pay to lessen the hardship caused by the tragedy. It's not a fortune, but it will provide some breathing space as workers search for new jobs.

But that's not going to be easy. With the farm economy in desperate straits, people with the money to develop new enterprises in rural Saskatchewan are few and far between.

Sitting in the living room of the Ryans' home, just two blocks from where the couple worked, it's hard to perceive the extent of their personal disaster. The colour television plays softly and the coffee pot sits full in the kitchen, just as it would on any weekend morning, but today is Friday—the first Friday without a job.

"I could probably get work on a farm this summer," Terry says, "but then what?"

With just one of their three children still at home and few debts things could be worse, admits Mavis.

"But we will have to probably move—possibly to Saskatoon. Our problem is: who will buy our house here?"

The financial problems for the family are painfully real, but there are other considerations, such as the loss of their friends and neighbours, that ride heavy in the couple's hearts. Country dances and visits to the local pub or curling rink could be a thing of the past for the Ryans and others who might be forced out of the community.

The fire in Cut Knife burnt more than a building and 25 jobs; for some it incinerated a way of life.

Maryanne McKenzie says that each day on the trap line brought something new.

Memories of Life in the North Bring Smiles

She smiles and the lines on her face move across smooth skin like ripples bringing life to a placid lake. The old lady is speaking in the soft delicate tones of her native Cree, remembering the trap line her family worked along the Churchill River.

Maryanne McKenzie is 88, and full of tales of her young years in the north. She grew up in the remote community of Stanley Mission, moving deeper into the wilderness every year with the coming of trapping season. This closeness to the wilds taught her to appreciate the earth; to live in harmony in a place where nature ruled with both velvet and iron gloves.

It was a time of innocence. A time when the way of life was good, she says. Maryanne speaks through her daughter, Sally Milne, who translates her mother's conversation for me.

"She enjoyed the outdoor life. They had a very independent lifestyle. They had their own gardens and literally lived off the land. The only imported item that was essential to them was tea," Sally laughs.

She picks up on the memories of those good times. Like all daughters, she enjoys the exploration of a life seen through her mother's eyes. The reconnection with her mother brings continuity to the cycle of life.

It's Sally's home at Napatak, about 10 kilometres south of La Ronge, where we are meeting. Maryanne McKenzie sits in her chair watching the flames slowly lick at the open door of the big wood stove in the centre of the living room.

"Mom says she remembers sitting around campfires with the old women of that time, watching them do their birchbark biting," Sally tells me.

Maryanne likes the memories of the winters best. That was when her family would leave the relative comfort of Stanley, where they spent the summer months, and head north to their trapper's cabin near Otter Rapids.

The soft tones of her native language are barely audible as she talks about canoe trips on pristine lakes, teepees, abundant beaver, and the darkness of a vast, silent forest that held no fear for this youngster of the north. But life everywhere brings challenges, and pain in life is unavoidable.

"Her dad died just before she was born, so my grandmother had to raise my mom and her older sister alone. They had to work to survive, chopping their own wood and working hard on the trap line."

Maryanne also recalls the Spanish flu outbreak in 1918–19 that killed more than 50,000 Canadians. The influenza epidemic devastated northern communities in Saskatchewan. Because the adults in her family were laid up sick and unable to chop wood, she and her sister had to pull out garden fence posts to use as firewood.

"Both sets of her grandparents died in the outbreak, and she remembers seeing the trading post manager's sleigh being used to pick up the dead from the little houses in the community," says Sally.

It seems a harsh life by today's standards, but it was a life in which boredom played no role.

"She says every day brought something new. You'd never know what you would catch on the trap line. Some days a lynx, a mink, a fox; sometimes nothing," Sally explains.

In the evenings there was little opportunity to relax. Skinning operations took up long hours, and the women would also cook the beaver, lynx, or muskrat meat. Chopping wood, mending fishing nets, making jackets, mukluks, and moccasins filled in any empty hours.

There was also time to tell stories about the old days when the spiritual grandfathers watched over the Cree. They would talk of special places such as Rattler Creek, where people went out on vision quests, hoping their fasting and aloneness would bring the right spirit force to help guide them on their psychic journey.

These days, Maryanne, a widow for the past eight years, lives with her grandson in her own home in La Ronge. She lives a quiet life now, but still keeps very active, according to Sally.

"She knits lots, for everybody. She'd still chop her own wood if we'd let her."

Maryanne doesn't understand the language, but she smiles at the other smiles in the room. Her bright eyes are alive with fresh thoughts of 88 years' worth of days gone by.

Wangchuk: "By the time most people have reached 40 or 45 or whatever, they often find they are struggling with life."

Buddhist Teaches
—— the Value of the Present ——

"First, you'll notice a sense of peace when you're in Wangchuk's company," said my friend about her teacher of yoga and meditation. "Then you will connect this serenity to the deeper understanding of life she has reached. There's a quiet wisdom in her."

Heavy-duty stuff for someone like me, who's more attuned to fridge-magnet philosophy than any in-depth perusal of higher disciplines. However, such an interesting invitation could not be passed up.

So there I was in Wangchuk's simple apartment, drinking honeyed black tea and feeling, sure enough, the peace of the Buddhist nun's company and her home. Wangchuk, the name she took when she was ordained in 1974, was not the name she was born with back in war-torn Germany.

I can imagine that it wouldn't have been the most comfortable time in Hamburg back then, to have your childhood awakened by the crash of bombs and your playgrounds echoing to the sound of gunfire.

Later—long after she moved to an ambitious accounting career with a Toronto import/export company—she discovered a deep need to look inside herself to find more meaning to life. She turned to Gestalt Therapy as the vehicle of self-discovery.

For a number of years she used the therapeutic system as a pathway to exploring and healing, but then came the heady '60s with its hippy movement riding roughshod over the social mores of the time. North American psyches rebounded with an increasing acceptance of eastern thought and religion.

For some neophytes the touch of sandal and robe would prove only a temporary phase, an experiment with a fashionable unknown; for Wangchuk it would be the start of a lifelong and ever-expanding connection with Buddhism. Talking with her, some 30 years from her first introduction to Buddhism, you feel the strength of her chosen path in every line and curve of conversation.

While her spiritual path has been extensive, her physical travels have been equally broad. She has made many visits to remote parts of the planet—from Guatemala to India—to learn and teach. She came to Saskatoon in 1990, and soon attracted new students.

Through yoga and meditation, her students settle on an inward journey that can lead to a personal mind/body awareness which deepens understanding about life. "Meditation and yoga are all about increasing your awareness," she says with an enigmatic smile. "Through awareness we can avoid acting out our negative social conditioning, we can tap the unconscious mind and increase our capacity for love and compassion."

It's not an easy process. The mind is tricky, and efforts to cease the flow of chatter and thought racing around it takes training and practice. Learning yoga and meditation requires discipline. But there are incentives. She says her students have a natural curiosity, an urge to look inside. They have lots of questions, she says, "about what life is." They have become tired of keeping busy and being totally absorbed with mundane trivialities. They want to bring deeper meaning into their lives. "By the time people have reached 40 or 45 or whatever, they often find they are struggling with life. What used to work for them, to get them through the day, doesn't work anymore." They are tired, and tired of being tired, she says. The goals they had set themselves in the material world have been reached or have become unobtainable, or they no longer see them as important.

"They feel empty. At first they try to deal with this by increasing their already busy schedule, leaving no time for nagging unpleasant thoughts to break through. They might numb themselves through work, alcohol, or drugs, but eventually they will stagger to a halt, emotionally drained or physically battered."

Wangchuk says this life stage could turn out to be the most critical for the individual. It could be the point when the mind turns away from fruitless excess efforts at obtaining "success" to focus on an inward journey, a noble quest of discovery of self and others.

"We are a product of our conditioning. At this stage people begin to question the authenticity of the conditioning they had taken for granted for so long."

Planning for the future, dwelling on the past; few of us spend any amount of time really experiencing the present, and yet that is where we are all the time. It's in the present that the simple acts of a daily life can become a part of a rich tapestry. Calming the mind and body through yoga and meditation can develop the skills required to live in the present, she said.

My friend had been right. I had enjoyed my time with Wangchuk. After I'd finished my tea and bade my goodbyes to her, I headed into the swirl of the evening rush-hour traffic. With thoughts dwelling on the directions we select in life—paths taken and ignored—I journeyed towards home, my mind a little more conscious of who was holding the steering wheel.

Face-to-face with a Siberian tiger.

Zookeeper Is Nuts about Animals

The Siberian tiger looked me straight in the eye and licked his chops. The massive cat obviously had taste. It was a beauty, but then again most of the animals I saw in the Moose Jaw Zoo and Recreational Park that day held strong appeal. After the first 20 minutes, I thought it was just a case of me going animal crackers, but I found out I'm not the only one who's nuts about wild animals.

At the time of year when most of us are slapping money into RRSP funds, Lew Oatway is cashing them in to put food into the bellies of cougars, tigers, and a host of other exotic creatures. His hard-earned life savings are being used to finance the Moose Jaw zoo he's taken over.

The zoo used to be operated by the provincial government but was leased out to a private company in 1988. Lew managed the operation most of last year and took over the long-term lease from the original shareholders in January. Appropriately, his company is called Zoolew Inc.

Sinking all your life savings into a zoo does not exactly rank up there with blue chip stock and treasury bills as a prime income generator. And considering the zoo in question has always been a big money loser, you might wonder why Lew and his wife, Lana, are focusing their lives, not to mention their wallets, on such a cause.

"We plain and simple fell in love with the animals," says Lew, 57. "It was a case of walking away from a problem or facing it square on."

Oatway says both the government and the private operators lost money operating the facility. The zoo's financial picture did not exactly attract the entrepreneurial spirit. There was a danger the zoo would close, and its 150 animals be dispersed, he says. But the year the Oatways spent running the zoo had its effect; they both became very close to their charges.

"It would have been a tragedy if it had closed. The closest zoos comparable to Moose Jaw's are in Winnipeg, Calgary, and Minot. That's a long way to go to visit animals of this class," Lew says.

While the couple feels confident about the outcome of their investment, the expenses of running a zoo can be crippling. With three full-time and two part-time employees, the monthly payroll is a big item.

I turn away from the increasingly interesting stares coming from the Siberian tiger as Lew tells me about the number of mouths he has to feed. The couple faces quite a grocery bill.

"It costs plenty to feed the animals. We go through about 1,600 pounds of meat every week plus a tonne and a half of fish a year. Luckily quite a bit of that is donated," Lew says.

With $40,000 of their life savings already swallowed up by his animals, you might expect Lew and Lana to be looking for big rewards at the end of the day. Not so.

"Zoos are historically money losers, but we're banking on our long-term strategy for bringing the place back into the black," says Lana.

Their strategy involves hands-on management, community and volunteer involvement, a high-tech computer-linked educational program for youngsters, as well as upgrading present facilities.

"This year we have set up a brand-new interpretive program for visiting school tours," she says.

Lew explains that a big booster for the zoo is its recent joining of the International Species Information System (ISIS). That organization links more than 200 North American zoos, allowing these facilities to exchange information on their stock and even lend species out between member zoos.

Lew, who was originally hired by the former operators to develop a championship golf course, was as surprised as anyone to find himself operating the zoo.

"Two years ago if you would have said I would be running a zoo, and have sunk this much money in it, I would have told you to have another drink."

However, fate, a bundle of cashed-in RRSPs, and spending long days looking after a fair cross-section of the animal kingdom can play strange tricks. These days Lew and Lana are figuring their zoo holds a strong potential for fulfilling not only their dreams but the dreams of other animal lovers.

Wib Walby of Wilkie has spent almost 40 years playing Santa Claus and says every year has been an adventure.

Career Santa
—— Is Still a Busy Man ——

There's the lists that have to be checked twice, the long white beard that needs its regular combing, and the red suit to be sent to the dry cleaners; Wib Walby is a busy man this time of year. I had first met Santa, I mean Wib, about a half-dozen years ago. Back then he was celebrating more than 30 years of passing out gifts, bouncing kids on his knees, and all the other ritual activity that a good Santa Claus is supposed to perform.

And they don't get much better and more dedicated than Wib, a Santa who is approaching his 71st Christmas and still eagerly donning the red suit. He hasn't changed much. His health is still pretty good, outside a couple of "little" strokes he had not so long ago.

He still has lots of air in his lungs for the occasional Santa sounds, except earlier this month he needed all his ho-ho-hoing to clear his sore throat. And while he might downplay a stroke as a little quirk of nature, Wib's much beloved wife, Eileen, will attest that he can sure wring his hands bemoaning a common cold.

"I got this damn cold, always happens when we come back from the lake this time of year," he told me.

Wib and Eileen have a cabin at nearby Jackfish Lake. That's where they spend about 80 percent of their time. But this close to Christmas, they always head back to town to spearhead the seasonal celebrations. To Wilkie and surrounding area, Wib Walby has been Santa Claus a very long time.

Wib's a jolly man, but his lasting relationship with Santa began in tragic circumstances. He was a soldier during the Second World War and stationed in England when one Christmas he volunteered to act as Santa for a London school. It went over well. Wib's role as Santa might have ended with that first appearance but for a German bomb that hit a nearby school the very next day after his performance.

"It killed a whole bunch of little kids. It was devastating seeing the bodies of those innocent children," he recalled.

The shocking scene, the smiles and laughter from the day before, the connection with his role as Santa: he really doesn't know the whys, except that the profound effect produced a career-Santa. Wib would make the role his seasonal vocation after his return to Canada.

Being Santa was always an adventure for Wib. He even had his very own sleigh, but pulled by a horse with wooden antlers and a red light-bulb hooked to a contraption on its nose. Not that invention was restricted to just the animals in the act. Before he grew his own magnificent beard, Wib himself had to be doctored up. The local undertaker had to paste his face with an unknown but powerful solution, to hold on his fake beard.

"I don't know what chemicals were in the stuff he used, but it sure made me goofy."

For a long time Wib was Wilkie's town foreman. In that capacity he could be counted on in a pinch to be Santa's helper when the weather did not cooperate.

"We'd sometimes get a sudden thaw and the snow in town would melt. I'd take the town truck out in the country and get a few loads of snow to spread along Main Street so my sleigh could get around."

He's a touch slower these days, he admits. This Christmas he hasn't been attending so many activities. There was the school, of course, and a few children's parties, but you get older, and the kids, well they seem to stay the same, he smiles.

"I love the kids—in fact that's why I do it—but the little darlings can be a bit tiring."

In the old days, back 10 years and more, it was nothing to put in 20 visits on Christmas Eve. His nightly tour took him all around town: the Legion, Elks, and Kinsmen children's parties, the schools, private homes, and the developmental centre, where the children who were physically and mentally challenged had a special place in Wib's big heart.

"I guess it's all about bringing smiles to the kids' faces. I like that," he said, looking over the top of his Pickwick spectacles.

He looked sad. I wondered if he was thinking back to that cold day in the London school yard, and if he saw the faces of those kids who would never again see Santa.

James Friesen never has to worry about being snowbound on his farm.

This Farmer's Innovation
Is Plane To See

There's no doubt that when it comes to improvisation and invention Saskatchewan farmers take a back seat to nobody. You only have to take a ride in James Friesen's home-made snow-plane to sample the talent and mechanical expertise of this Rosthern-area farmer. In the farming community, necessity has often proved the mother of invention. During pioneering days, with little formal mechanical training and even less money, prairie farmers depended on their imagination to survive.

Friesen's snow machine is an example of that initiative. The powerful lightweight machine was built in 1980, and it's still running strong over the moguls of snow blanketing the summerfallow around his farm.

"I built it for emergency use back when the children were going to school. It came in handy when the school bus couldn't make it out to the yard," the 61-year-old farmer explains.

When the snowdrifts piled up, blocking the access road to his isolated farmhouse, Friesen just fired up his snow-plane and drove his two youngsters to meet the schoolbus at the highway, three kilometres away.

It's still in perfect shape. A turn on the electrical starter brings to life the six-cylinder engine mounted on the back of the steel pipe frame. The propeller, painstakingly hand-fashioned by Friesen out of a solid piece of birch, blurs into action, moving the sleek craft gracefully across the fields.

An air-cooled engine, reconditioned from a scrapped 64 Corvair auto, powers the machine. Friesen has accelerated the snow-plane up to about 60 kilometres an hour—once. Fast speed is not something he recommends.

"It could go faster, but I want to get to my destination in one piece." At about 40 kilometres an hour, it's a smooth ride. The three skis mounted under the aluminum skinned vehicle have springs salvaged from a 1950 Ford. Friesen used the same source for the snow-plane's single headlamp. A steering wheel rescued from the aging Corvair makes sure direction control poses no problem. Total cost of the machine came to less than $700, although he doesn't count his labour in that figure.

Both his children have long since left home, and these days the schoolbus no longer needs to make the trip to his farm, five kilometres east of Rosthern. There's not a lot of emergency need for his four-seater snow-plane. However, once in a while, when the fancy takes him, he powers up the craft and takes a long spin across his farm.

"I only use it a few times a year just to make sure it's still working," he says.

*Wilf Badger is accustomed to the loneliness
that goes along with long distance trucking.*

The Lonely Life of
—— a Long-distance Trucker ——

The night sky was dark against the darker forest and the northern lights spilled like paint down a canvas. It was two in the morning and Wilf Badger slept silently, unseeing and uncaring of the vivid display on the other side of his windshield.

He had woken an hour earlier, wide-eyed and alert. It was the dream where his semi was rolling backwards that had made him leap from the comfort of his bunk in the plush padded cave behind the driver's seat. He laughed at the realization that, even after 16 years of long-distance hauling, he could have nightmares about forgetting to apply a parking brake.

He had pulled out of the Northern Resource Trucking depot on Millar Avenue just a dozen hours earlier. A burly hand had controlled the large steering wheel like a china dinner plate while the other, with the precision of a conductor, moved intricate patterns with the gear stick through the 15 forward gears of the 400-horsepower silver behemoth.

His was a delicate task. He was hauling propane—15,000 kilograms of it—to Cameco's Rabbit Lake mine, 800 kilometres north of Saskatoon. The 37-hour round trip, however, was old hat to the veteran trucker, who often makes it three times a week in the winter.

The torpedo-like trailer hitched behind his tractor held enough propane to drive about 1,700 barbecues through a season of family cookouts. As a heat source for the giant mill that processes the uranium ore, it will last only a few days.

It was four hours since he had edged into a pull-off around 130 kilometres north of La Ronge to grab some sleep. Badger had brought his cargo more than halfway to the isolated mine site.

He had manoeuvred between gear stick and his seat to climb into the bunk in the sleeper at the back of the cab. "If I'm not awake already, get me up at two," he had called out of the comfortable darkness. His passenger, who was at that moment gingerly folding his body into the driver's seat and looking uncertainly at the solid steering wheel that was to be his pillow, nodded agreement. If only one of us sleeps tonight, better it be the driver, he thought.

Black jackpines stretching towards the sky surrounded and swallowed up the mighty Kenworth. Even bristling with the soft glow of its parking lights it was no match for the brilliant stars and the light show of the gods erupting overhead. For the passenger, the rumble of the killing diesel engine and the steady eyes of the 20-or-so dials that spread across the dash, were the only reminders of factories, business, and commerce. Badger slept. It was a lonely spot.

Maybe that's why long-distance truck drivers hold great store in coffee breaks. Condemned to a life of exile, their stops are less for the hot coffee than a ritual for intimacy. Conversation and discussion are at a premium for a driver alone in the confines of his cab and who wants to keep his sanity. The cafes and restaurants that dot the more familiar and busy highways to the south are no strangers to the north.

They become meeting places for the transient truckers who have swallowed more than enough yellow lines for a while. Coffee, a couple of cigarettes, and a sharing of experiences are something to look forward to for the driver facing a narrow but endless ocean of asphalt and gravel.

Badger's first stop on this trip had been at a roadside cafe between Prince Albert and La Ronge. Squeezing his 400 horses and modern-day wagon beside a logging truck and another massive vehicle bearing the large, ominous signs *Explosives*, he pulled the Kenworth to a stop.

A couple of workers and a few truckers leaning over their Cokes, coffee, and french fries discussed the varying quality of both roads and politicians. Such was the intertwining of ideas and interconnecting thought patterns on the two subjects. It was difficult to distinguish descriptions. Was the highway crooked or the politician potholed?

The roadside cafes are great places to catch up with news. Is such and such still hauling potatoes in Alberta? Has so and so lost his truck to the finance company? Does what's his name have his licence back yet? Is you know who back with his wife?

After a half-hour, Badger gets up and pays for his coffee but not before buying a new pack of Players Filter—more companions for the long trip north. He moves out into the cold parking lot and into the shadow of his truck. He produces a small hammer and wanders around his vehicle tapping the tires, checking the pressure. A soft tire could result in a flat, or worse, a blowout. Not good news in northern temperatures.

The coffee was a distant memory. Now reality was that he was awake at Kilometre 130. It took five minutes to get back into his clothes and check his mirrors before the hiss of released brakes and the sigh of his air-cushioned seat meant the rig was back on course on Highway 905. Travelling down the road, following the tunnel of light produced by his headlights, Badger was lost in his own thoughts. "What are you thinking about, Wilf?" was the question from his passenger.

He looked surprised. There's no radio reception this far north and the cassette deck with its mountain of country music tapes was silent. "What do you think about when you are alone?" the passenger asked again.

"I think about my life, from beginning to the end, or to now anyhow," he answered. He divorced five years ago. The life of a trucker can be unforgiving to a marriage, he said. Away from home for long stretches, sometimes only arriving back in time for a shower before heading down the road again, the trucker needs someone with more understanding than the average human can muster.

He has children and he thinks about them a great deal. Three daughters, all grown up and gone from home. The old plastic binder holding his log book and travel documents is a reminder. "It's my baby's," he said, pointing to the school-age signature on its cover. His youngest daughter, who is now a mother, is still his baby. There was a son, an only son, who died about five years ago. He had been 17. "I think a lot about him when I'm on the road," Badger said softly.

He thinks about his own childhood and the farm where he grew up near Kamsack. One day he would like to get his own farm with a few head of cattle. It's possible, he figures, and it would get him from behind the wheel eventually. Not that he doesn't enjoy driving.

After a few days in the saddle, I get tired of it, he tells you. But absence is a great anchor for the heart. "If I haven't driven for a few days and I see a truck busting loose down the road, I'm anxious to be back at it."

Highway 905 snakes its way up the northeast side of the province, providing a lifeline to small communities and settlements as well as the gold and uranium mines that trucking companies such as Badger's serve. Driving in the north is different. The roads are rougher, narrower, and much harder on a vehicle, Badger explained, with weather conditions providing the wild card.

Speeding past a gully along the deserted gravel road, he pointed out the spot where his truck slid into the ditch last year. It was where he would spend the next 17 hours in -45° weather waiting to be pulled free. His hand points ahead. This is where a semi smashed into the tow truck that was just about to pull a vehicle from the ditch. And then there's the loneliness of being behind a wheel in the north.

But, he says, his eyes brightening, there's good reason to be in the wilderness. The money's good—he'll be paid $250 for driving the round trip. And the game and wildlife that occasionally patrol the roads can be an exciting break in the monotony. Once, a whole pack of wolves tried to out-distance his truck after he had surprised them on a blind corner. Bear sightings are common, although the trucker says the albino bear he saw north of La Loche a few years ago is still etched deeply in his mind. "I didn't tell anyone for the longest time because I didn't think they would believe me," he said.

Ever popular and romantic in trucking songs, the CB radio is but a brief and tenuous lifeline to the outside world. With only a short range—often only a few kilometres—the radio still serves to connect two human souls passing in the night. A glimmer of headlights and Badger's hand has reached to the microphone above the windshield before the vehicles have even met. There was just time for a few words. A couple of questions about traffic or obstacles up ahead and the words dissolve into electronic crackles.

With less than a hundred kilometres to go to complete the trip to the minesite, Badger is silent. The warm glow of a cigarette shone from his left hand as the truck rocked over the road like a ship at sea. Badger stared ahead into the horizon as the Michelins pounded over the highway towards a pale new dawn.

John Kaminski erected a sign to thank God for healing.

Farmer's Faith Park
Gives Thanks

Alone he'd built the big sign, complete with a full-scale plywood cut-out of Jesus, to spread the message that God's power is not to be trifled with; yet the hoodlums shot it up anyway.

There's a deep but benign sigh from John Kaminski. He scans the bullet-scarred placard that he'd laboured over only a few years ago and turns to look from the hillside, towards the snow-covered fields stretched out below. Pointing to a grove of poplars, black and skeletal against the bright snow, his voice rises in enthusiasm.

"I built a park here, you know, with a miniature church, swings, benches, and those things ... you know, where you can cook hot dogs. And there was this treehouse, not an ordinary treehouse, but one of the biggest ones I'm sure that was ever built, that I put up in them trees there."

John had established the park on some of his farmland and erected the sign on the hillside above it as a way of thanking his God for the healing that had come to him more than 20 years ago. It was his way of spreading the message of the Lord and to provide a cosy recreational spot for a rural picnic.

Not every tourist came to relax, though. A few not-so-well-meaning individuals came to vandalize. The miniature church, the sign, and the treehouse were substantially damaged, but the vandals couldn't wreck the builder's faith.

"I did my part, and I suppose it's not my fault that there're hoodlums in the world. I'm glad that I was given the chance to do the work," he says.

His expression of gratitude was born out of adversity. Two decades earlier his body had been a real mess. Arthritis, rheumatism; he says the doctors were never sure about all that was troubling him. What he knew, however, was that the pain in his body and joints had left him virtually paralyzed with agony. For five years or more John's condition had gradually deteriorated to the point where he had all but given up hope of any relief. His farming operation near Bruno had been put on hold, and he had resorted to renting out his land because physical work had become an impossibility.

"I couldn't escape the pain. I had two mattresses with a sheet of wood between, but it hardly helped at all. Then one day a friend suggested I go see a woman in Saskatoon who used prayer to heal people. Now, I wasn't very religious to speak of, but when things are this bad you'll try anything."

So John ended up at a Saskatoon prayer meeting, a last resort to surrendering to his illness. As he returned home that evening he brought with him the same pain, but also a little hope things might change. After three days he found his faith and he lost his pain.

"It was a miracle. A few days after my visit to Saskatoon I went for a walk to try and take my mind off the pain and as I walked the pain ... well, it just left me, it went away. All I could think to say was, 'Praise the Lord.'"

And that's just what he's been doing ever since. But John wanted to put some visual expression to his feelings and prayers, and he took to sign painting with the vigour of the truly converted.

"I painted signs on my barns and other buildings so that others might turn to the Lord, that they could find the answer in his word. The healing is out there for everyone, you just have to believe," he says, a wide smile crossing his face.

He's 69 now. Since his "born again" conversion and his regular twice-a-week attendance at local prayer meetings, he has seen many other healing miracles: sickness cured, pain removed. He says these miracles cost nothing, you just have to look in the right direction.

These days he has his pension and lives a simple life on a five-acre spread on the edge of Humboldt. Reading the Bible from cover to cover, finding the answers to life in the words of the age-old testaments, and once in a while putting paint to board as he writes out on signs some of the messages of hope for others to see.

He's happy, too, and you can see a contentment in his bright eyes as he flips through the pages of his Bible.

"You know, when your body is wracked with pain, all pulled and twisted inside, it's hard to think straight. But when that pain's gone you can see clear, like it was morning or something. I wish everybody could have that feeling, and they can, you know. That's what my signs are all about."

V.A. 'Dode' Terry has worked a trap line for 63 years.

Trapper Answers
the Call of the Wild

That night he peeled the potatoes and tended the sizzling pork chops, not once stepping on the dead fox at his feet. It would have been nimble work in any kitchen. In the confines of the cluttered trapper's cabin, with only the light from a coal oil lamp to work by, it was especially impressive. Meanwhile, thanks to focused footwork and able hands, V.A. 'Dode' Terry continued his monologue of 63 years of experiences on the trap line, neither scorching the food nor trampling the freshly caught fox.

"They said if BS was snow, then that man would have been a blizzard," Dode said of a young fellow trapper he once knew. "Anyways, from then on everyone called him Snowball," he laughed, leaning over the wood stove to turn a nicely browned pork chop.

Reminiscing with 83-year-old Terry is a luxurious collision of the historical with the practical. His eyes and limbs are still willing to brave the hardships and the isolation of the trap line—a sure sign of the strength of the human spirit.

Every year he spends a number of two-week stints working his trap lines on the 466 square kilometres in his fur block territory, beyond the north end of Tobin Lake. When he's had enough of the fumes, from his snowmobile and his own cooking (although, during the long weekend I visited with him, he proved a great cook), he heads back to his wife, Pearl, and their family farm, about 20 kilometres north of Nipawin. Sometimes the well-known trapper visits schools across Saskatchewan to tell younger folks about his trapping days.

"Of course, trapping in the early days was very important. I had to take it much more seriously. Hell, it was the trap line that paid for my farm, built the buildings, and bought the machinery. Now it's more or less a hobby."

Down in a small Nebraska town, his given name at birth had been Virgil. Since that time, he's covered a lot of ground, moving around several states before heading to Saskatchewan in 1925 as a young teenager. Somewhere along the way he shed his name.

"I don't know where it came from, but since childhood it's always been Dode. Anyone who calls me Virgil I know is a long way from these parts."

The family homesteaded near White Fox after a difficult journey from the state of Washington. But when the cut-down Model-T Ford— carrying two parents, six kids, and a dog—finally arrived, their relief at the end of their trip was short-lived.

"There wasn't a spot cleared of anything. Trees, bush, and mosquitoes were everywhere, but at least we had a homestead. That's more than we had before."

During those harsh years of heavy-duty bush clearing, Dode and a friend would go off into the bush to trap. It was a practical diversion.

"There was nothing else to do for recreation. And in those days, if you wanted to go to a movie or a dance you needed money. You had to go catch a weasel or something to get the dollar to get in."

By the time he was 21 he left with his chum to set up a trap line about 100 kilometres northeast of Nipawin, near the present site of the E.B. Campbell power station (originally named Squaw Rapids). After building a log cabin, they spent the winter and spring trapping for "anything and everything," from beaver to timber wolf.

"I remember we came home for Christmas that year. It was a three-day walk. After the holiday we went back out and didn't set off home until the middle of May. We came back on the Saskatchewan by homemade rowboat, fighting rapids and ice all the way." You don't have to listen to Dode for too long to figure out the potential dangers the trap line can hold for even the most experienced bush person.

"Ice is a bugger, especially in spring. I never trust it. I've fallen through a couple of times and damned nearly drowned or froze to death. Somehow, I've always managed to make it to shore and get a fire going."

Even water in its unfrozen state holds enough danger. A few times, Dode and a partner have upset canoes in frigid waters.

"Always managed to grab a branch or a rock, or I might not have been here cooking these pork chops today. I'd never tell the wife about these happenings until long after. No good scaring her." He toppled a small hill of hashbrowns on my plate.

His campsite nowadays is pretty luxurious compared to the past, doubling as a lodge mainly for American hunters in the fall and spring. When the hunters arrive, Dode acts as cook and general factotum, maintaining the radio set, cabins, shower shack, and electric generator.

"It's a change. The hunters come and go and mostly they're good fellas. But you can't beat getting out on the snowmobile on a crisp morning, and travelling the trail looking for what might have got itself caught in the traps."

Some time ago he published a small book of poems, *Tales of a Trapper*. Written over the years in the aloneness of his cabin next to the Torch River, the poems were an attempt to reflect the drama— sometimes humour—of life on the trap line.

His descriptions—of trees snapping in the cold, vivid northern lights, howls of timber wolves, and crystal-bright stars—are the other side of Dode Terry. In conversation, the ever-practical trapper mostly seems to regard nature as something that's, well, just there.

Once in a while, however, he does surprise you. Like the moment when I'd plucked up courage to ask if there was a spiritual side to him. After all, anyone who writes poetry can't be all practical.

Zeroing in on the last of the two pork chops he had allotted himself, Dode chewed the query over in his mind.

"Well, I'll tell you this. You can't spend as long as I have in the bush and still be an atheist.

"Now, if you want more hashbrowns you better go get 'em from the pan yourself. I've got to skin that fox before bed."

Robert Way hopes to preserve the old Coteau View School.

A Former Student Hopes
to Save His One-room School

The one-room prairie schoolhouse has pretty well bit the dust these days. Once an important part of Saskatchewan's rural landscape, it has gradually disappeared along with quarter-section farms and horse-drawn sleighs.

Little is left to remember these educational centres, if you can use such a grandiose term for the trim little buildings that once dotted the countryside from Assiniboia to Meadow Lake. You might find the odd marker of those bygone days. Often it's a cairn. The inscription that usually beings "On this site stood ... " is generally the only reminder of the laughter, chalk dust, and the mischievous kids—the students—who learned about a bigger world beyond their own borders.

But out in a field near Elrose, there's more than just memories of the days when education was delivered in one room, where a half-dozen grades would converge in varying degrees of concentration on maths, geography, history, and spelling during the same class period.

The Coteau View School, all one room of it, still stands proudly in the soft summer wind. The Coteau Hills, which gave the school its name, lie to the south, hazing out in the distance, far away from the greening wheat fields that edge the four-acre plot of school grounds.

"It's been here since 1948, through rain and shine. I can't go past the place without getting goose-bumps at the memories," says former student Robert Way, 39. The local farmer wants to preserve the structure, maybe make it into a museum eventually. His modern farmhouse bungalow stands less than a mile down the road from the aging school building. The days of Way's youth at Coteau View are distanced only in time.

"We'd maybe have 14 students from Grades 1 to 6 in the school, but it was a place where we learned how to work independently," he says.

Another small one-room school building stood a few metres from this structure. It was home for the Grades 7 to 10, but was later torn down for lumber.

Coteau View was a happy place, recalls Way. A spot where education included gopher hunting, moonlit hockey games, and the learning of the importance of friendship in rural culture.

"There was so bloody few of us you couldn't afford to pee anybody off. We had to learn how to get along with everybody."

At the beginning of summer he and some other neighbours got together to honour the memory of the old school, which had graduated its last student back in 1965 when the doors finally closed. More than 150 former students and their families showed up to reminisce.

Way explains the school building was originally built in 1928 and moved to its present site 20 years later as local school divisions amalgamated. Less than two decades later, a declining rural population led to the demise of Coteau View, and the students were bused to Elrose about 25 kilometres to the northwest.

It was the end of an educational era for Way and school life was never quite the same. The one-room school, however, had put roots deep into his life. Even when he went to university, the benefits from those learning days in rural Saskatchewan played their part.

"I think the self-discipline and study habits I learned in those days went a long way in making me who I am today," he says.

And so it was for many of the people of the Prairies. Before the necessary coming of computer rooms, language arts, and semester systems, the eight-metre-square one-room schoolhouse played its part in creating Canada.

Listening to lessons echoing across the hardwood floors and gazing at world maps that still showed coaling stations for merchant ships, their students moved uncertainly, but bravely into a new world.

Bill Marshall sports his new bee beard.

They Make a
Honey of a Beard

While it's somewhat of a ticklish pastime, there's no doubt the bee beard competition was one of the premier attractions at the second annual Tisdale Honey Festival this month. Safely screened off by a glass partition in the Tisdale Recplex curling rink, a few hundred spectators came to watch seven competitors from as far away as B.C. grow beards from swarms of live bees.

It takes experience and a steady nerve, but the participants in this year's competition had no shortage of either. With $2,700 in prize money at stake, they had no trouble sitting perfectly still while their assistants groomed some pretty fancy beards out of the thousands of bees clustered on each contestant's chin.

In the end the winner turned out to be Byron Janzen, a working beekeeper from Carrot River who managed to shape an almost perfect beard from the collection of honey bees he had brought along from his farm. His stylish performance won him about $1,800, the winner's purse.

The event takes quite a bit of preparation, explains Bill Marshall, a local honey producer and another contestant in the competition. Each bee beard competitor is allowed as much as four pounds of bees in forming his individual beard.

That adds up to 18,000 to 20,000 bees per contestant, estimates Marshall. With the seven competitors in the glass and plastic enclosure, that means as many as 140,000 of the buzzing critters were let loose for the 20 minutes each participant was allowed to form a beard.

Marshall attracts his bees by taping a small box containing the queen onto his chin. The bees swarm around their queen and Marshall's assistant, his son Mike, uses a credit card in an attempt to form the bees into an attractive beard.

One or two stings are fairly common over the 20 minutes it takes to shape the bee beard, but as a bee keeper, Marshall says he gets stung many more times than that every day during the honey extraction season.

"The main problem is the heat. That many bees on your face and you can imagine how hot it can get, not to mention the itching," he laughs.

Judges at the event were marking contestants on the volume of bees on the facial area and the beard's appearance, particularly its uniformity and balance. After the performance, Mike and the other contestants are called into action to remove the bees from the faces of the competitors. Mike uses a vacuum to suck the bees off his dad's face. Other performers use cones, knocking the passive bees from the face into the cone.

After removal, the bees are rehoused in the travelling hive and taken home to get busy doing the job nature really intended them for: producing honey.

Domremy farmer Russell Hanson cuddles his pet lynx.

Farmer Breeds Lynx
for Sale

I enjoy the company of cats, but I think Russell Hanson beats my affection for felines, hands down. How else could you explain the fact the Domremy farmer allows his three pet lynx to hurtle around the family living-room to their hearts' content? Bouncing off chesterfields, racing across the carpet, and whirling around coffee tables, his three bundles of joy work off their wild enthusiasm amid the tranquil domestic setting of Hanson's farmhouse, about 120 kilometres northeast of Saskatoon.

All this would be distracting enough if the cats were of the cute Siamese persuasion or possibly nice, soft Persians. However, when you

144

consider these babies weigh in around 15 kilograms a piece, you can imagine life with Duke, Fluffy, and Tuffy can be a real handful.

I was talking to Russell about this very fact, when one of his cats—Fluffy, I think—decided to give me an affectionate hug. This would have been fine except the little darling believes in giving his hugs on the run. After I regained my breath and Fluffy was distracted with a new, more forgiving toy in the shape of a tennis ball, I came to the attention of Duke.

Duke is the biggest of the three cats. A Siberian, this animal will reach about 40 kilograms by the time he is fully grown. Even at six months, this feline is no pussycat by ordinary standards, but a cheeky swat to the back of my head, with a declawed paw the size of a table-tennis racket, indicated he was just as playful as his smaller Canadian cousin.

"Rambunctious, aren't they?" my genial host smiled. "They're a real joy to have around, but they do get pretty active."

I was thinking this is what it must have felt like at ice level during the Russian hockey team's fight with the Canadian players, when there was a muffled crash from the basement.

"One of them must have got into some more mischief," said an unconcerned Russell, engaging in some friendly wrestling with Duke.

About four years ago the cattle farmer first became involved with lynx. A badly injured back had forced Russell to look for ways to diversify his farming operation. Breeding lynx, to sell mainly to zoos or to other breeders, looked promising. He purchased his first breeding pair from Alberta, and now has almost 40 of the beautiful creatures in his care. While most of the animals remain wild, and are kept in stout metal cages outside, the entrepreneur has bottle-fed and house-trained several of his lynx.

"You have to take them away from their mothers after they are about nine days old. Besides bottle-feeding them, you have to treat them like any other baby; you even have to wipe their bums. It's quite a job."

Inside a few weeks, the young kittens are house-trained and, like regular cats, will use kitty litter, albeit the industrial-strength variety.

"But they can't stay long inside, it's far too hot for them. These animals are built for the cold, so I keep them in cages in the yard."

Later, eating a diet of ground chicken—feathers and all—the lynx grow rapidly into healthy adults. Kittens raised by their mothers will fetch about $500, while lynx raised domestically can sell for more than $1,300.

"Siberian lynx are more rare and valuable and can sell for up around $2,000," Russell says.

His diversification program has expanded to four wolverines, which he's attempting to breed—a difficult, but financially rewarding task.

"I have already sold two of them to a Montana wildlife photographer for $14,000."

Ultimately Russell says his dream is to have his own zoo on the family farm featuring primarily cats. I asked him if these creatures would be better off in the wild than prowling around zoo cages. His thoughts on that question are clear and emphatic.

"People think all wild animals should be free, but let me tell you, there's no such thing as freedom out in the wild. My lynx might be restricted in their movements compared to in the wild, but they have full bellies and they sleep with both eyes closed."

Age may have slowed Ron (left) and Chum Edwards a bit,
but retirement isn't a word in their vocabularies.

Brothers Still Feel
—— at Home on the Range ——

One of the two ranchers quietly rolls a cigarette; the other stares through the dim shadows of the log home, towards the window and beyond, to the line of rumpled hills that swell up to the horizon. The knolls and gullies of this prairie scene are as familiar to Chum and Ron Edwards as the back of their weathered hands. The men have been part of this landscape all their lives and they are still an active component, continuing to work their 1,200-hectare family ranch near Findlater.

"We've definitely slowed down," Ron explains, swivelling his eyes away from the bright scene on the other side of the window to the shadow-veiled interior of the small, cluttered room.

At their age—Chum is 87 and Ron is 78—you'd think the two brothers should be thinking more about traditional retirement pursuits than operating their 300-head cattle ranch in southern Saskatchewan.

Try telling them that.

"We're feebling up now, but you can't expect any darn thing else at our age," sighs Chum, the elder of the two brothers who jointly work the family spread, about 70 kilometres northwest of Regina.

"It's a darn nuisance. The mind wants to get up and go but the body don't want to go on along. But we've been here all our lives."

Born and raised in the Arm River Valley, the two ranchers have lived the prairie's hard and soft seasons. They have sweated and frozen their bodies and furrowed and lined their brows riding horses and running cattle herds across the rolling panorama of this part of Saskatchewan. It was a job they were born to.

Their grandfather, Charles Edwards, moved to Saskatchewan in 1883, settling in the Moose Jaw area, homesteading on a vast and very empty prairie landscape. At the time of the Northwest Rebellion he freighted supplies between Moose Jaw and Saskatoon for the government forces.

"Grandpa got to see Riel after he was captured and on his way to Regina," Chum says casually, crumpling his cigarette into an ashtray and popping a small wedge of snuff into his mouth.

The two brothers said that drought eventually forced the fledgling homesteader to move into the Qu'Appelle Valley, only to find the ravages of prairie fires pushing him once again. This time Grandfather Edwards put down permanent roots in the spring-fed Arm River Valley.

"They were tough times then. The elements seemed to be always agin' you," remembers Chum. "We had a prairie fire in these parts that started the other side of Watrous and came at us on a 14-mile front. By the time they'd managed to put it out, that fire had travelled 80 miles."

In 1939 they buried Grandpa.

"Thirty below and blowing terrible cold. We had a bitch of a time digging his grave. We had to put up grain doors to act as a windbreak. Otherwise he wouldn't have been the only one buried in that hole."

Chum and Ron's father, Jack, carried the family ranch into a new generation, building a new log cabin for his expanding family. That same cabin, built around the turn of the century, is still home to the two bachelor brothers.

"You have to remember in those early days neighbours were few and far between," Ron said. "The Mounties in Lumsden had their regular horse patrol pass through here. They'd often spend the night."

Sitting in his well-worn rocking chair, Chum rolls another cigarette and looks at the low ceiling of his minimalist home. There's no running water, no electricity, and no telephone. A spring near the barn supplies all their water, an oil stove provides heat, and a wood stove is used for cooking. Propane gas lights brighten the home.

"I do most of the cooking," Chum says. "I normally make the meals for the whole bunch that comes to help with the cattle's black-leg injections and other treatments, but I couldn't manage this year. My eyes are too bad."

His cooking is done in the ranch kitchen, a room pinched into the confines of the main floor. A larger living-room/dining-room takes up all the rest of the space. A farm-sized, vinyl-covered table occupies most of the floor area of the living-room, leaving space for Chum's rocking chair and a sofa, which Ron shares with a sleepy family dog during our conversation.

The room is crammed with almost 100 years of collected history of their ranch and district. Some rodeo pictures and a variety of elderly calenders decorate the walls. Books, papers, and ranching magazines are stacked up on cupboards and chairs, and a couple of ancient hand-cranked phonographs stare silently out of a dark corner.

"Yes, it's quite a while since those machines played anything," Chum says. "Diamond reproducer flew off some years back and you can't replace them. Used to like to play the old-time music. It was music you don't hear anymore, reminded me of better times when we were younger." His eyesight fails him nowadays. Keen eyes that once spotted straying cows against a distant horizon now focus more inwardly.

"I get around here pretty well, thanks more to my memory than my eyesight. It's so many steps to the wood pile, so many to the barn. I shuffle around pretty good, considering," Chum says.

A full-time hired hand does most of the hard physical work around the place, but Ron still breaks in horses and is more comfortable in the saddle than driving the farm half-ton.

"I still drive, but I don't like the city anymore," he said. "It's too much like hard work."

But the two have many friends and neighbours who continually drop by to shoot the breeze and discover some of the living history of the region. Both Ron and Chum have memories sharper than porcupine quills. For those privileged to share their time, they can reach into a storehouse of memories that paint pictures brighter and more vivid than any history book.

"Ah, we get lots of visitors. Sometimes it's hard to get anything done around here we get so many folks dropping in," Chum said, walking over to the window. "Just checking on the hired man out baling hay in the meadow aways. He's not been well, got a hacking cough—graveyard cough we used to call them—don't want him to overdo it."

The brothers agree it's been a hard life, but interesting so far. They have not travelled much. Ron's been out to British Columbia a couple of times and enjoyed the mountains and lakes.

Chum has no regrets.

"Maybe we've been foolish to end up living in this old house, but it's still pretty good and strong. Some of the modern houses are no hell as far as keeping the winter out, you know. I've heard of folks sitting around the kitchen table in those new homes and wearing Ski-Doo suits while they eat their supper, the wind's been screaming through walls that bad," Chum says, flourishing a newly rolled cigarette in the air.

The nip of the winter wind is not the only bite that's taken out of the quality of life down on the ranch.

"We've had a plague of mice this year," he explains, holding up an old newspaper, the most recent victim of rodent power. "The darned critters got into everything and almost drove us crazy, but we've survived it.

"I think that's what living here's been all about—surviving—and I think we've managed that. We don't have much but we don't owe a cent to nobody, and that's saying something these days."